The Sheffield

D0293505

HUMAN
RIGHTS

2008–2009 EDITION

PETER HALSTEAD

Orders: please contact Bookpoint Ltd, 130 Milton Park, Abingdon, Oxon OX14 4SB. Telephone: (44) 01235 827720. Fax: (44) 01235 400454. Lines are open from 9.00–5.00, Monday to Saturday, with a 24 hour message answering service. You can also order through our website www.hoddereducation.co.uk

If you have any comments to make about this, or any of our other titles, please send them to educationenquiries@hodder.co.uk

British Library Cataloguing in Publication Data
A catalogue record for this title is available from the British Library

ISBN: 978 0 340 96685 3

First Edition Published 2005
This Edition Published 2008
Impression number   10 9 8 7 6 5 4 3 2 1
Year   2012 2011 2010 2009 2008

Copyright © 2005, 2008 Peter Halstead

Hachette Livre UK's policy is to use papers that are natural, renewable and recyclable products and made from wood grown in sustainable forests. The logging and manufacturing processes are expected to conform to the environmental regulations of the country of origin.

Typeset by Transet Limited, Coventry, England
Printed in Great Britain for Hodder Education, part of Hachette Livre UK, 338 Euston Road, London NW1 3BH by CPI Cox & Wyman, Reading, Berkshire.

Contents

Preface   v

CHAPTER 1 **Introduction to human rights**   1
  1.1 Overview   1
  1.2 Human rights language   2

CHAPTER 2 **Human rights theory**   5
  2.1 Approaches to human rights theory   5
  2.2 The 'UN' approach   8
  2.3 A conceptual approach   10
  2.4 A contrasting or comparative analysis 11
  2.5 The rule of law   17
  2.6 General development of rights   20

CHAPTER 3 **The global regime**   24
  3.1 UN Charter and Declaration   24
  3.2 UN Organs   31
  3.3 The Covenants   37
  3.4 UN Conventions   40
  3.5 *Jus cogens*   49

CHAPTER 4 **Regional regimes**   51
  4.1 The regimes   51
  4.2 Europe   52
  4.3 The Americas   55
  4.4 Africa   60
  4.5 The Minsk Convention   63
  4.6 Arab Declaration and Charter   64
  4.7 Asia-Pacific forum of National Human Rights
      Institutions   66
  4.8 The Organisation for Security and Cooperation
      in Europe (OSCE)   68
  4.9 The European Union (EU)   70

CHAPTER 5 **Themes**   76
  5.1 Indigenous peoples   76

5.2   Abolition of slavery   78
5.3   Abolition of the death penalty   81
5.4   Genocide, crimes against humanity and war crimes   83
5.5   Humanitarian intervention and peace keeping   86
5.6   Apartheid   89
5.7   Truth commissions   92

CHAPTER 6 **European human rights**   **94**
6.1   The beginnings   94
6.2   The Council of Europe   97
6.3   European Convention principles   99
6.4   Types of Convention rights   100
6.5   Operating principles of the European Court   104
6.6   Other European Conventions   106

CHAPTER 7 **The operation of the Convention**   **108**
7.1   The Convention Articles   109
7.2   The Convention Protocols   122
7.3   Procedure   126

CHAPTER 8 **The Human Rights Act**   **127**
8.1   The European years 1950–98   127
8.2   Bringing rights home 1996   129
8.3   The Human Rights Act 1998   130
8.4   Current issues   135

CHAPTER 9 **Rights and remedies**   **148**
9.1   Skinning the cat   148
9.2   UN enforcement   151
9.3   Accountability   154
9.4   Impunity   154
9.5   Intervention   155
9.6   Regional enforcement   157

Index   161

Preface

The Key Facts series is designed to give a clear view of each subject. This will be useful to students when tackling new topics and is invaluable as a revision aid. Most chapters open with an outline in diagram form of the points covered in that chapter. The points are then developed in list form to make learning easier. Supporting cases are given throughout by name and for some complex areas the facts of cases are given to reinforce the point being made.

The Key Facts series is a practical and complete revision aid that can be used by students of law courses at all levels from A level to degree and beyond, and in professional and vocational courses. Largely as a result of the Human Rights Act 1998, this subject is now widely studied not only by students of law but by people interested in many other disciplines. This book deals with human rights in the UK and Europe, but its scope is considerably wider in that it addresses other regional regimes and global human rights, with chapters on underlying theory, rights and remedies, and a variety of specific themes.

Anyone who needs to study the subject for academic purposes, or who is interested in human rights and wants a comprehensive source or revision book, should find this book particularly helpful.

The law is stated as I believe it to be on 1st December 2007.

CHAPTER 1

Introduction to Human Rights

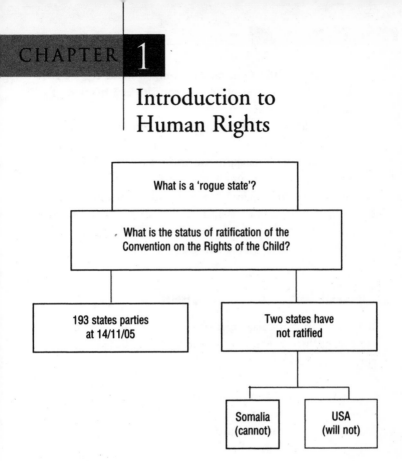

What is a 'rogue state'?

What is the status of ratification of the Convention on the Rights of the Child?

193 states parties at 14/11/05

Two states have not ratified

Somalia (cannot)

USA (will not)

1.1 Overview

1. There has been considerable interest in human rights in the UK in recent years since the Labour Party, then in opposition, promised to 'bring rights home' at the 1997 General Election by incorporating the bulk of the European Convention on Human Rights into domestic law, subsequently implemented by the Human Rights Act 1998.

2. This encouraged schools, colleges and universities and employers to give high priority to providing courses on human rights, where much of the emphasis has been on changes in UK law, and to a lesser extent on European developments.

3. Although the European regional human rights regime is advanced and successful, it only constitutes a fraction of the totality of human rights.
4. Whilst addressing UK and European concerns this book also provides a broader perspective so that students are introduced to the background and theory of rights, as well as the global system and regional regimes, thematic concerns traditional and modern, and rights and remedies.
5. Using this book both as an introductory guide and revision aid, students will obtain a broad understanding of the main aspects of local, regional and global human rights.

1.2 Human rights language

References to particular organisations and treaties should be clear from the context, but knowledge of the following commonly used contractions will be useful:

CEDAW	The Convention on the Elimination of all forms of Discrimination against Women
ECHR	May mean European Convention, Commission or Court of Human Rights, depending on the context
ECOSOC	(UN) Economic and Social Council
GA	(UN) General Assembly
HRA	Human Rights Act 1998
ICC	International Criminal Court
ICCPR	International Covenant on Civil and Political Rights
ICESCR	International Covenant on Economic, Social and Cultural Rights
ICJ	International Court of Justice
ICRC	International Committee of the Red Cross
ILO	International Labour Organisation
INGO	International Non Governmental Organisation
NGO	Non Governmental Organisation
SC	(UN) Security Council

UDHR   Universal Declaration of Human Rights
UN   United Nations
UNHCHR   United Nations High Commissioner for Human
          Rights
UNHCR   United Nations High Commissioner for Refugees

1.2.1 Glossary

Civil and political rights: first generation citizens' rights to
    liberty and equality.
Collective rights: the right of native aboriginal groups to have
    their rights as a whole protected, as opposed to an
    individual's right to a fair hearing, or freedom of worship.
Convention: a legally binding agreement between states,
    entered into voluntarily and enforceable only to the extent
    acknowledged by signatories, and used more or less
    interchangeably with the words 'covenant' and 'treaty'.
Covenant: *see* Convention.
Customary international law: in domestic terms, roughly the
    equivalent to common law, as opposed to treaties which
    can be compared to statutes.
Declaration: a set of non-legally binding standards to be
    observed by states.
Economic, social and cultural rights: second generation
    rights giving people rights to the material necessities of life,
    rather than to individual freedoms.
Environmental and development rights: third generation
    rights of mankind to have a safe and healthy environment,
    and for peoples generally to live in harmony.
Generational rights: a theory explaining in metaphorical
    terms the nature of human rights, particularly since the
    Second World War (see 2.2.2 following).
International Bill of Human Rights: the combined totality
    of the UDHR, ICESCR, ICCPR and its optional protocol.
Protocol: an addendum to a Treaty which modifies it, often
    used to incorporate optional provisions not acceptable to
    all states' parties.

Ratification: confirmation by a state's legislative machinery of adherence to a convention.

State: a territorial area occupied by a society that possesses the same government and accepts the same laws; states are mostly synonymous with countries.

Treaty: *see* Convention.

Westphalia, Treaty of: Peace Treaty between the Holy Roman Emperor and the King of France and their respective allies, signed in Munster, October 24, 1648, and taken to be the foundation of the modern system of independent nation states

CHAPTER 2

Human Rights Theory

Rights may be:
- civil
- political
- economic
- social
- cultural
- generational

Concepts of rights may be:
- universal
- inalienable
- interconnected
- Interrelated
- indivisible
- obligational, ie including responsibilities

HUMAN RIGHTS THEORY

Natural and human rights theorists include:
- Thomas Hobbes
- John Locke
- Rousseau
- Immanuel Kant
- Wesley Hohfeld
- Lon Fuller
- John Rawls
- John Finnis
- Jack Donnelly

Rights may be comparative or contrasting:
- universal/relative
- collective/individual
- positive/negative
- active/passive
- right/rights
- moral/legal
- natural justice/legal justice
- claim rights/liberty rights
- will theory/interest theory

2.1 Approaches to human rights theory

2.1.1 The 'UN' approach

1. There are many ways of theorising about or categorising human rights, the more usual being:
   - civil;
   - political;

- economic;
- social;
- cultural.

2. Modern human rights are built primarily on Western notions of individually based civil and political rights.
3. The Cold War (1945–89) brought out an alternative approach from the Soviet bloc, which preferred to emphasise collective economic and social rights.
4. The emergence of the Third World from colonial subservience after the Second World War led to advocacy for cultural and developmental rights.
5. There are analogies here to Karel Vasak's generational theory, discussed below.

2.1.2 A conceptual approach

1. Another method is to describe human rights as being:
   - universal;
   - inalienable;
   - interconnected;
   - interrelated;
   - indivisible;
   - obligational, ie including responsibilities.
2. The problem with using such descriptions is that they are sweeping, sometimes tautologous, and tend to ignore the practicalities of how human rights actually operate in the modern world, not really explaining what is meant by 'interconnected' or 'indivisible'.

2.1.3 A comparative or contrasting analysis

1. Often comparative or contrasting approaches are used, some of which overlap in meaning, including:
   - universal/relative;
   - collective/individual;
   - positive/negative;
   - active/passive;
   - right/rights;

- rights/freedoms;
- moral/legal;
- natural justice/legal justice;
- claim rights/liberty rights;
- will theory/interest theory.

2. This is a popular, albeit simplistic, comparative way of explaining the ideas behind human rights, because it focuses attention on specific but limited aspects of their nature, bringing out similarities and differences.

2.1.4 Writers and practitioners of natural and human rights

1. A common methodological approach is to consider individual writers, or to trace a line of philosophers who have contributed to the growth of particular strands of natural and human rights theory.

2. Such earlier European philosophers would include:
   - Thomas Hobbes (1588–1679);
   - John Locke (1632–1704);
   - Jean Jacques Rousseau (1712–78);
   - Immanuel Kant (1724–1804);

3. Twentieth-century and contemporary writers on human rights would include:
   - Wesley Hohfeld (1879–1918);
   - John Rawls (1921–2002);
   - John Finnis (1940–);
   - Jack Donnelly (1951–).

4. This chapter is about theory, but human rights are also often measured by the great 'practitioners', whose writings or political achievements were also influential, eg:
   - Mohandas Karamchand (Mahatma) Ghandi (1869–1948);
   - Eleanor Roosevelt (1884–1962);
   - Nwlaon (Nelson) Eoliklalla Mandela (1918–);
   - Aung San Suu Kyi (1946 –).

2.2 The 'UN' approach

2.2.1 Why 'UN' approach?

1. Labelling civil, political, economic, social and cultural rights as the 'UN' approach is:
   - shorthand to summarise the main thrust of the way that mid- and late-eighteenth-century rights theory developed into twentieth and twenty-first-century international and regional rights regimes;
   - 'regimes' means quasi-legal systems with limited enforcement mechanisms that are frequently overlooked or ignored for political and economic reasons.
2. The forces that drove the early movements towards human rights had some of their origins in seventeenth-century English events, but were primarily fuelled by the American and French revolutions in the late eighteenth-century.
3. Karel Vasak's generational theory reflected this; propounded in 1979, it provided a metaphorical explanation of how rights came to be formulated, suggesting how they might be recognised as continuing to be developed, and providing a useful tool for explaining how rights mean different things according to the context.

2.2.2 Karel Vasak's third generation rights

1. Vasak's generational theory suggests the development of human rights is (metaphorically) equivalent to the French revolutionary slogan *liberté, egalité and fraternité*, giving us first, second and third generations of human rights development.
2. *Liberté* provides first generation rights, which are:
   - civil and political in nature;
   - designed to protect citizens from excesses perpetrated by the state;
   - fundamentally negative in nature eg articles 3–21 of the Universal Declaration and the ICCPR;

- in practice, comprise freedoms such as religion, speech, fair trial, etc.

3. *Egalité* characterises second generational rights, based on social, economic and cultural factors. They are mostly positive and would:
   - include employment and family rights as contained in articles 22–7 of the Universal Declaration and the ICESC;
   - require states to institute programmes that would benefit the individual.

4. *Fraternité* means solidarity, implying group and collective rights such as those of peoples to self-determination and to promote their own economic, social and cultural development, much less evident in the conventional global human rights regime.

5. Specifically these would relate to rights to:
   - development;
   - peace;
   - a healthy environment;
   - ownership of the common heritage of mankind (eg the seabed);
   - communication.

6. This moves beyond consideration of the individual *per se* and extends human rights to community and interactive areas and issues, reflecting globalisation trends.

7. The essential characteristics of third generation rights are the need to impose:
   - joint obligations on all states;
   - further obligations wider than those on states, extending to international actors such as INGOs and transnational corporations;
   - obligations on peoples as a whole, rather than on individuals.

8. Vasak's theory helps to explain the process of 'concretisation' of rights from theoretical idealism prior to the American and French revolutions, to practical implementation after the Second World War.

9. An example would be the 1986 UN Declaration on the Right to Development, together with various documents, charters and treaties providing support for the emergence of fraternal rights to peace and a healthy environment.

10. The use of the generational metaphor is not meant to imply the demise of previous generations and their subsequent replacement.

11. There is debate about whether solidarity implies:
    - a quantitative or qualitative shift in the nature of human rights;
    - the birth of entirely new rights, or extensions of the old, ie are the joint aspects and responsibilities of developmental rights of a different nature to previously recognised individual rights?

12. Opposition to Vasak's theory has been based on differing suppositions:
    - human rights are individual and enforceable by law, but solidarity rights are collective and not capable of legal enforcement;
    - that attempting to add these to the rights currently accepted in the International Bill of Human Rights will dilute the efficacy of those fundamental rights and freedoms.

13. Vasak's theory is an elegant theoretical approach to understanding the origins, development, implementation and possible future trends of international human rights, but is not meant to be interpreted as a literal application of the French revolutionary slogan.

2.3 A Conceptual approach

1. The use of the word 'inalienable' is usually taken to mean that human rights cannot be:
   - bought and sold;
   - inherited;
   - given away;

- otherwise disposed of by:
  - the person who holds the right in question;
  - that person on someone else's behalf (eg his or her child).

2. For example, a person does not possess the power to sell or give him- or herself or his or her children into slavery, servitude or forced labour, even voluntarily.

3. Interconnected, interrelated and indivisible rights apply to all human beings by virtue of their very humanity, and mean that the various rights and freedoms contained or referred to in many documents and treaties are:
   - interdependent;
   - not to be ranked in order of perceived importance;
   - not to be qualified or reduced any further than is clearly provided for in particular instruments (most rights being qualified rather than absolute, as can be seen in the European Convention on Human Rights).

4. 'Obligational' means that rights are connected to correlative responsibilities and are not simply free-standing claims that individuals or peoples can call upon in a vacuum eg Hohfeld's analysis (see section 2.4.7).

5. 'Universal' is also a commonly used word, the contrast here usually being with (cultural) relativity, dealt with in the next section.

2.4 A contrasting or comparative analysis

2.4.1 Universal or relative human rights?

1. The universal theory of human rights posits the idea that there is an international paradigm that must be applied uniformly across the world.

2. This is the theory behind the United Nations' Universal Declaration and the twin international covenants that together make up the International Bill of Human Rights.

3. Cultural relativism is the counter-argument that human rights, some of which may be desirable but not essential,

are not uniform or necessarily based on individual civil and political rights, but vary across the world according to:
- differing cultural practices;
- the reality of huge variations in economic and social development in different continents, countries and societies.

4. A significant weakness of the cultural relativity approach is that it is often used by ruling politicians or elites in states where they are protecting particular interests and the general population are unable freely to express their views.

5. An important weakness of the universal argument is that although it proclaims itself to be God-given and self-evident, the fact remains that human rights are not universally respected, observed or applied and the existence of God is a matter of faith rather than proof or evidence.

2.4.2 Collective or individual rights?

1. The English, American and French traditions particularly influenced the modern world rights system, which tends towards the universal and individual, reflecting a mature democratic background and considerable personal and material security.

2. Others, coming from different and less affluent cultures, argue that collective rights which aim to protect groups of people or complete societies are more important, as for example the need to protect:
- *children* in the global context more than an individual's right to (say) freedom of speech;
- *workers* who may be exploited by powerful transnationals to produce goods for lucrative markets and affluent consumers;
- *subsistence dwellers* whose need for the basics of life – clean water, food, health care, education and safety from attack or worse – might appear more cogent than freedom of thought or belief.

2.4.3 Positive or negative rights?

1. Positive human rights are not universally acknowledged. They arise from Rousseau's continental tradition under which the state should provide equality, education, health care and the means of earning a living and supporting the family; alternatively these are sometimes referred to as welfare rights.

2. The negative approach stems more from the English and American tradition, which tends to believe that rights comprise things that government should not be allowed to do to the individual; documents illustrating this include Magna Carta, and the English and American Bills of Rights.

3. Examples of both positive and negative approaches are found in modern global and regional regimes.

4. An alternative way of classifying *negative* rights is as active or passive:
   * 'active' implies ability to do what one chooses;
   * 'passive' comprise rights to be exercised at will.

2.4.4 Right or rights?

1. Originally what are now recognised as human rights (however defined) were called natural rights, and arose out of man's need to try to explain his place in the universe.

2. Later natural law theory became more refined and sophisticated, and tended to be founded on a monotheistic view of life, but still only implying relatively few principles.

3. The modern approach changed the emphasis from natural to human rights, and started to provide long lists of individual rights possessed by or attributed to human beings, eg specialist treaties relating to children, women, slavery, genocide, etc.

2.4.5 Moral or legal rights?

1. In theory the distinction is simple:
   - legal rights exist in legal systems, enforceable within states and between states, but only where they are bound by treaty or under legitimate international compulsion;
   - moral 'rights' are better described as moral claims, as they are not *legally* enforceable under either system.
2. If rights are accepted as being objective, of high priority and universal, it is implicit that compliance with them is mandatory and the conclusion can be drawn that they are moral in origin.
3. However, if they are subjective and culturally relative, then universal compliance will not apply and observance of them would depend on legal rules within particular jurisdictions.
4. In practice, human rights are made to apply (albeit patchily) in both the moral and legal spheres, although mostly imposed by legal machinery.
5. Moral imperatives drive the search for justice following such international crimes as ethnic cleansing or genocide, evidenced by the Rwanda and former Yugoslavia tribunals, and now the ICC.

2.4.6 Natural justice and legal justice

1. Some of the origins of human rights can be found approximately 2,500 years ago in Greek philosophy through notions of natural law and justice, connected but not identical ideas.
2. Natural justice could be found in innate conscience-driven ideas of fairness, rightness and wrongness; it is subjective and differs from one person, society and generation to the next.
3. Legal justice stems from legal rules imposed by particular states or leaders of societies on those within their power and jurisdiction, and stems from legal positivism, ie the laws and rules that are imposed (posited) by those holding

or granted power to rule over others.

4. In England these legal positivist ideas were developed in the nineteenth century by Jeremy Bentham, John Austin and John Stuart Mill, and in the twentieth century the concept of justice as fairness was promulgated by John Rawls.

5. Legal positivism did not have much to say about human rights as they are now understood, although Mill's ideas on utilitarianism suggested that the greatest good for the greatest number would contribute towards human happiness, albeit at a price.

2.4.7 Claim rights and liberty rights

1. These originate in Wesley Hohfeld's theory published in 1919, attempting a thorough classification of what he identified as four differing types of right:
   • liberty rights;
   • claim rights;
   • power rights;
   • immunity rights.

2. In recent years there has been a tendency to integrate these into two composite types:
   • liberty rights;
   • claim rights.

3. Claim rights are thought to be of primary importance and are defined as rights that are owed a duty, to which there may be positive or negative claims:
   • a positive claim right applies to a particular thing (ie a good or service) which someone else has a positive duty to provide;
   • a negative claim right is one with which you have to prevent someone else interfering, eg one threatening your health or wellbeing.

4. A further sub-division is that claim rights can be held either against a person (*in personam*) or a thing (*in rem*).

5. Liberty rights are things you can do which are not

prohibited, so they are mainly negative; eg no one can stop
you from exercising your liberty right to dine at
the Ritz.

6. The corollary is that no one has a positive duty to make it
possible for you to be able to afford to do so; thus liberty
rights provide the ability to be free to do something
without willing the necessary means.

2.4.8 Will theory or interests theory?

1. This involves the question of whether human rights are
self-evident, or need justification.

2. If they are self-evident they would arise from an empirical
set of facts perceivable in the world, from which arise
duties and obligations that humans recognise and observe.

3. However, the validity of human rights in the real world
requires them to be made choate by means of legal
machinery, which is itself based upon tangible and
justifiable principles.

4. Interests theorists believe that the main purpose of human
rights is to further basic human interests and needs,
identifying the things that humans need to live purposeful
lives in a state of wellbeing.

5. This viewpoint is represented by John Rawls who identifies
the basic forms of human goods as being:
  • life and its capacity for development;
  • acquisition of knowledge, as an end in itself;
  • capacity for recreation;
  • aesthetic expression;
  • sociability and friendship;
  • practical reasonableness;
  • capacity for intelligent and reasonable thought processes;
  • religion, or the capacity for spiritual experience.

6. Earlier philosophers such as Thomas Hobbes put forward
their own practical reasons why interests should form a
foundation for human rights.

7. Cultural relativists criticise this approach, as the basic forms of human goods are not universal and what would pass in, say, the Sudan or Myanma (Burma) would be unacceptable to an American or European.

8. Will theory argues that the validity of human rights in philosophical terms is based on the human need and capacity for freedom.

9. Hart took the view that all men had an equal right to be free, and that all the things people wanted to do could be achieved if they had the one thing necessary, ie freedom to exercise their will.

10. Others, such as Ronald Dworkin, Henry Shue and Alan Gewirth have developed versions of will theory that in different ways base human rights on the idea of personal autonomy.

11. One problem facing this approach is that not all humans have (sufficient) autonomy (eg children and people with mental or physical incapacity), so if will theory is right, how could they claim human rights when they are unable to exercise the will that would bring them into play?

2.5 The rule of law

1. The purpose of the rule of law is to legitimise government by showing that it is impartial, fair and must be obeyed, whether or not you agree with a particular political regime or specific provisions.

2. The essence of the rule of law is that authority is subject to and constrained by law, comprising the following elements:
   - no one should be punishable except for distinct breaches of the law;
   - no one is above the law;
   - everyone should be subject to the jurisdiction of the ordinary courts (*Entick v Carrington* (1765));
   - punishment should be in the ordinary courts and in the manner prescribed by law;

- there should be no arbitrary or random exercise of power;
- discretionary exercise of power is common in modern government but its extent should be clearly defined and limited.

3. Where there is no written constitution:
   - there should be judicial review of administrative action;
   - constitutional principles are contained in the common law and a few legislative provisions, such as Magna Carta (1215) and the Bill of Rights (1689).

4. The incorporation into domestic UK law of most of the European Convention by the Human Rights Act 1998 provides additional support for the rule of law.

5. The rule of law does not stand in isolation, and is analogous and connected to other rights principles:
   - accused persons should not be placed in double jeopardy;
   - all people should be treated equally, eg no separate rights of trial for certain individuals, such as peers, although this does not preclude specialist tribunals for particular classes of case or person;
   - everyone is innocent before the law until proven guilty;
   - law, especially criminal law, should not be retrospective;
   - there should be separation between executive (governmental) and judicial functions, part of the doctrine of the separation of powers;
   - the content of law should be clear and readily accessible;
   - everyone should have access to affordable legal advice and representation.

6. One of the concerns of human rights today is the extent to which some of these hard-won traditional safeguards are being whittled away by government, abetted by Parliament, in response to and using as justification terrorist threats eg:
   - a person who has been acquitted of an offence could not under common law be charged again, as that would place him or her in 'double jeopardy' (at risk twice) and

he or she could plead *'autrefois acquit'* (already cleared);

- the principle was restricted by the Privy Council in *Connelly v DPP* (1964), which held that this did not prevent the accused from facing a different charge based on the same facts;
- the Criminal Justice Act 2003 Part 10 which came into force on 4 April 2005 now permits some retrials eg:
  - when modern science may now secure a conviction using evidence that was not probative at the first trial;
  - where the person acquitted has subsequently confessed eg Billy Dunlop's murder in 1989 of Julie Hogg, eventually leading to his conviction in 2006;
- nevertheless it erodes an important principle that previously protected people from having a perpetual threat hanging over them.

7. It is obvious that not all of the other principles enumerated above as comprising aspects of the rule of law are entirely applicable to the English legal system eg:
   - internment flouts the idea that everyone is innocent until proved guilty;
   - retrospective law is sometimes imposed;
   - application of the doctrine of separation of powers is only partially valid in the UK and the overwhelming power of modern governments to get their way mostly unhindered by weak and compliant parliaments exemplifies this;
   - much of the content of modern law, and in practice the ways in which it applied, are not clear, open and readily accessible (eg use of speed cameras to raise revenue, criminalising motorists);
   - not everyone has access to affordable legal advice and representation.

8. Prior to the:
   - European Convention;
   - right of individual application to the European Commission; and
   - enactment of the Human Rights Act;

Judicial review was an important part of the direct application of the rule of law to protect human rights in the UK, eg where a compulsory purchase order was wrongly made, adversely affecting citizens' property rights (*White and Collins v Minister of Health* (1936)), or where a mother wanted to challenge provisions that undermined her view of family life (*Gillick v West Norfolk and Wisbech Area Health Authority* (1985).

2.6 General development of rights

1. The expression 'human rights' came into general use after 1945, although probably first used by Henry Thoreau in the previous century, and at their simplest they can be defined as rights belonging to individuals by virtue of the fact that they are human.
2. Rights can be traced in Western philosophy to Stoic natural law doctrines, ideas that originated with Zeno of Citium, the Stoics teaching that there were pervasive laws of nature and man's conduct should therefore be measured in accordance with those laws.
3. Roman law developed the idea of natural law into a law of nations, whose universal provenance fitted in neatly with their conquest of the then known world and their desire to foster colonisation, trade and settlement.
4. In the Dark and Middle Ages the Catholic Church through theologians such as St Augustine of Hippo (354–430 CE) and Thomas Aquinas (c.1225–74 CE) developed these ideas for its own purposes, distinguishing man-made laws and those of God, but 'rights' had a very different meaning from that of modern times recognising, for example, the legitimacy of holy wars and slavery.
5. With the Renaissance (end of the fourteenth century CE to about 1600 CE) and Treaty of Westphalia (1648) began the modern notion of sacrosanct states in which various populations worked out their relationships to their rulers.

6. Later in the Age of the Enlightenment (seventeenth and eighteenth centuries CE), the growth of knowledge encouraged a more rational and scientific approach to rights, with people starting to base their beliefs on empirical methodology and observation rather than solely on nature or God.

7. Revolutions in Europe and the Americas brought practical expression and effect to the development of rights, albeit with resistance from those who believed that rights should depend on laws made by rulers, and not on rhetorical nonsense on stilts, as Jeremy Bentham put it.

8. Dreadful experiences in the first half of the twentieth century put paid to most general ideas that rights came from God:

   • Marxism taught that rights could only be claimed by revolution.
   • Liberalism taught that rights had to be turned into universal norms and where practicable made enforceable.
   • The Cold War demonstrated that power blocs will cynically use different versions of rights to further their own political and economic interests.
   • States emerging from colonialism refused automatically to accept pre-conceived versions, Western or modified, preferring their own cultural versions.

9. In the early twenty-first century, in the post-Cold War era, the next stage of development of human rights is taking place, with general acceptance that some human rights are universal, although:

   • agreement by some states is grudging and half-hearted;
   • there are very few, if any, states where human rights are always placed first and foremost and which never allow political and economic means to justify the end;
   • there is equivocal and restricted agreement as to which rights should be accorded universality.

10. Examples of this limited universalism include:

   • the Convention on the Elimination of Discrimination Against Women 1967;

- the United Nations Convention on the Rights of the Child 1989;
- the latter is perhaps the most widely accepted human rights convention, with 192 states acceding to the treaty, and only the US and Somalia recalcitrant, but even these conventions suffer from many 'blanket' reservations by acceding states parties.

11. Despite that fact, there is worldwide mistreatment of children including:
   - slave labour and enforced servitude;
   - child soldiers;
   - failure to provide basic health care and elementary education;
   - ethnic cleansing;
   - child prostitution;
   - trafficking.

12. So the fact that governments nominally accept the modern universal norm, and do not want to be seen denying its tenets and implications, does not mean that they agree to establish an effective enforceable global regime or to be bound by aspects of it that do not suit their purposes.

13. The rationale behind this reluctant acceptance of human rights remains vague and diverse, with different states at different times relying on ideas that include the:
   - divine;
   - ethical;
   - moral;
   - legal;
   - culturally relative;
   - socially contractarian;
   - redistributive;
   - utilitarian.

14. These, and other approaches, can be linked to the varying theories of rights discussed in this chapter and although there have been encouraging post-Cold War developments, these are counter-balanced and sometimes negated by the

increasing uncertainties facing the world in the twenty-first century.

15. In particular, the issue of terrorism and human rights in the post-9/11 world is of crucial importance, posing stark contrasts between the fundamental aims and purposes of the principal protagonists:

- international terrorists, whose objectives may be assisted by elevation of criminal activities into what governments describe as 'the war against terrorism', thus implying some officially recognised status;
- civil rights movements or organisations, whose objectives are to maintain, protect and enhance freedoms that have taken centuries to wrest from oppressive governments;
- governments themselves, which have legitimate vested interests in protecting their populations whilst at the same time exaggerating risks and dangers, in order to enhance their own positions.

CHAPTER 3

The Global Regime

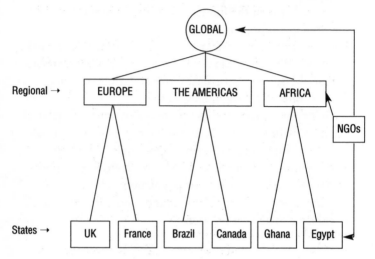

3.1 UN Charter and Declaration

3.1.1 Principles, ideals and motivations

1. The global human rights regime established after the
   Second World War had a number of underlying principles,
   ideals and motivations, including the need for:
   - an urgent response to the recent horrors and atrocities;
   - a framework broadly based on civil and political ideas of
     what human rights should be, derived mainly from
     English, American and French ie the Allies' history
     and sources;
   - strengthening international criminal law.
2. This chapter deals with global human rights in the context
   of international law, although many breaches of human
   rights occur within individual states.

3. Ideas for an effective global system of human rights were circulated during the war because:
   - the failed League of Nations had omitted adequately to address them, although there had been a system of minority rights protection that tried to avoid conflict in Europe;
   - in part this failure sparked the idea of protecting individuals as a way of preventing the development of tensions that could lead to armed conflict;
   - the emerging extent of Nazi atrocities required the definition of new crimes, together with machinery to tackle them.

4. It was impossible to obtain complete agreement on all matters that might have been included in an ideal scheme, as the following timelines show:
   - 1945 – UN Charter established the 'club rules';
   - 1948 – UDHR expressed generally accepted but unenforceable aspirations;
   - 1966 – ICCPR and a separate ICESCR covenant were approved;
   - 1976 – the covenants entered into force, becoming together with the UDHR the International Bill of Human Rights;
   - 1989 – Optional Protocol on Abolition of Death Penalty.

5. Another example is the international criminal law regime:
   - 1945–6 Nuremberg tribunals;
   - 1946–8 Tokyo trials;
   - 1993 Former Yugoslavia tribunal;
   - 1994 Rwanda tribunal;
   - 1998 International Criminal Court (Rome Statute);
   - 2002 ICC actually came into existence;
   - 2007 US continues to refuse to accede or support.

6. Both timelines illustrate how long it can take to bring projects to fruition when international agreement is needed and influential states such as the US refuse support.

3.1.2 The UN Charter

1. There were proposals to incorporate a bill of rights in the UN Charter and although (as exemplified above) this was not done:
   - Article 68 provided that ECOSOC would establish commissions in economic and social fields to promote human rights;
   - the UN Commission on Human Rights was established in 1946.
2. In the Charter there are merely exhortatory references to human rights, and even Article 56 in which all Members 'pledge themselves' is an unenforceable obligation.
3. The Preamble, second paragraph, said that the peoples of the UN were determined to reaffirm faith in fundamental rights, in the dignity and worth of the human person, and in the equal rights of men and women and of nations large and small.
4. More important substantive provisions include:
   - Article 1(3) which expresses some of the broad purposes of the UN, including promotion and encouragement of human rights and fundamental freedoms without distinction as to race, sex, language or religion, perceived as being an element of cooperation between states in solving international problems of an economic, social, cultural or humanitarian character;
   - Article 13(1)(b) refers to the initiation of studies for the purpose of making recommendations into the promotion of international co-operation in the economic, social, cultural, educational and health fields;
   - Article 55 provides for the promotion of higher standards of living, full employment, economic and social development, with progress and solutions to international economic, social, health, cultural and educational problems, all in order to create stability, wellbeing and peace;

- Article 56 reinforces this, members pledging themselves to take joint and separate action in cooperation with the UN to achieve those objectives;
- Article 62(2) enables ECOSOC to make recommendations to promote human rights based on studies or reports to be presented to the General Assembly, Member States, and specialised agencies;
- Article 68 empowers ECOSOC to set up commissions in the economic and social fields to promote human rights, and such other commissions as may be required for the performance of its functions.

3.1.3 The Universal Declaration of Human Rights

1. The original idea was that the UDHR would be followed by a single convention containing comprehensive provisions that states would ratify, incorporating the:
   - civil and political elements in Articles 1–21;
   - economic and social rights in Articles 22–8;
   - duties in Articles 29 and 30.
2. Ideological differences early in the Cold War precluded this, so in 1952 it was decided to proceed via two separate routes, the ICCPR and ICESCR, agreed in 1966.
3. The UDHR is perhaps the single most important human rights document ever produced because of:
   - its timing and global context;
   - the influence it has had on subsequent human rights documents and regimes;
   - the fact that although it is a declaration and not a treaty, many people believe it has acquired the status of customary international law.

The Preamble

1. This recognised the inherent dignity and inalienable rights of all human beings which need to be based on freedom, justice and peace, and the (then) recent barbarous acts that had outraged mankind's conscience.

2. It stated that the UDHR would strive to set a common standard of achievement to be brought about by education in order to promote and eventually secure universal recognition and observance of human rights and fundamental freedoms.

Civil and political rights

1. Article 1 states that all humans are born free and equal in dignity and rights, are endowed with reason and conscience, and should act towards each other in a spirit of brotherhood.
2. Article 2 entitles all humankind to the rights and freedoms contained in the Declaration without distinction of any kind, but specifically race, colour, sex, language, religion, political or other opinion, national or social origin, birth or other status.
3. Article 3 says that everyone has the right to life, liberty and security of person.
4. Article 4 prohibits slavery, the slave trade and servitude.
5. Article 5 prohibits torture, cruel, inhuman or degrading treatment or punishment.
6. Articles 6–11 deal with fair trials requiring:
   - everyone to be recognised as a person before the law;
   - equality without discrimination before the law;
   - effective remedy by national tribunals in cases of violation of fundamental rights;
   - absence of arbitrary arrest, detention or exile;
   - full equality to a fair and public hearing by an independent and impartial tribunal;
   - presumption of innocence, guarantee of defence, no retrospective law.
7. Article 12 requires absence of arbitrary interference with privacy, family, home or correspondence.
8. Articles 13–15 grant:
   - freedom of movement and residence within borders, and the right to leave;
   - the right to seek asylum from persecution abroad, but

not for non-political crimes;
- the right to nationality and not arbitrarily to be deprived thereof.
9. Article 16 gives adults the right to marry freely and have a family.
10. Article 17 provides the right to own property solely or jointly, and not arbitrarily to be deprived thereof.
11. Articles 18–20 deal with beliefs and how they can be expressed, meaning freedom of:
- thought, conscience and religion, and the right both to change and manifest them;
- opinion and expression, and to seek and impart information;
- assembly and association without compulsion.
12. Article 21 provides the right to take part in government, to have equal access to public services, and to periodic and genuine elections held by universal and equal suffrage with secret ballots.
13. Article 22 gives the right to social security and the rights that provide dignity and free development of personality, within each state's resources.

Economic, social and cultural rights
1. Article 23 states that everyone has:
- the right to work;
- free choice of employment with good conditions;
- equal pay for equal work:
  - all so as to provide sufficient remuneration for dignified family existence;
  - backed up by the right to join a trade union.
2. Article 24 stipulates:
- reasonable limitation of working hours;
- sufficient paid holidays to allow for rest and leisure.
3. Article 25 provides for:
- an adequate standard of living for health and wellbeing to enable sufficient food, clothing, housing, medical and social services, which should lead to;

- security against unemployment, sickness, widowhood, old age and other circumstances beyond the individual's control.

4. Article 26 provides for:
   - free and compulsory education, at least in the elementary and fundamental stages;
   - further education generally available and equally accessible to all on merit;
   - full human development of personality and respect for others, with parental choice.

5. Article 27 allows for free participation in community cultural life and the right to share in artistic and scientific advancement, subject to protection of intellectual property rights.

6. Article 28 states that everyone is entitled to a social and international order in which the rights and freedoms set forth in the UDHR can be realised.

Duties

1. Article 29 states that everyone has duties to the community in which alone the free and full development of personality is possible, but they:
   - must be subject to limitations in so far as they are necessary to secure recognition for the Declaration's rights and freedoms;
   - cannot be exercised contrary to the purposes and principles of the UN.

2. Article 30 provides that nothing in the Declaration can be interpreted to imply that anyone – state, group or individual – is entitled to do anything contrary to the aims and objectives of the UDHR.

Status

1. The then newly-formed UN Commission on Human Rights under the chairmanship of President Franklin D Roosevelt's widow Eleanor Roosevelt, decided to work towards a declaration rather than a treaty, to secure as rapid and widespread approval as was possible at the time, and the fact that it was:

- an international UN statement gave it moral and political importance;
- less than a treaty but more than a recommendation meant it had potential growth capacity to become binding under customary international law.

2. It was to:
   - include civil, political, economic, social and cultural rights;
   - be short and inspirational;
   - go a long way towards universal acceptability.

3.2 UN organs

3.2.1 UN Human Rights Council

1. In the UN hierarchy the Commission on Human Rights (the Commission), established in 1946, was inferior to the General Assembly and ECOSOC, but was significant for human rights, having:
   - 53 member governments elected for three-year terms by ECOSOC;
   - a chairmanship rotating between the main political and geographical groups, sometimes resulting in states with dubious human rights records such as Libya holding the chair.

2. Because of dissatisfaction with the Commission it was decided in 2006 by General Assembly Resolution 60/251 to replace it with the Human Rights Council, a subsidiary body of the GA.

3. Reasons for criticisms of the former Commission and its eventual demise include:
   - some members had poor domestic human rights records, including the People's Republic of China, Cuba, Zimbabwe, Russia, Saudi Arabia, Pakistan and Libya;
   - in 2004 Sudan had been elected to the Commission uncontested, despite extensive ethnic cleansing in Darfur;

- the US was frequently at odds with the Commission, failing to get itself re-elected between 2001 and 2003, and finding itself out of favour with rights abusers and European states because of US opposition to the ICC.

4. Responsibilities of the replacement Human Rights Council include:
   - promotion of universal respect for the protection of all human rights and fundamental freedoms for all, without distinction of any kind and in a fair and equal manner;
   - addressing gross and systematic violations of human rights;
   - applying principles of universality, impartiality, objectivity, constructive international dialogue and co-operation;
   - promotion of human rights education and provision of a forum for rights dialogue.

5. Although the resolution is fairly detailed there are uncertainties over how well the new arrangements will work, with interim continuance of the Sub-Commission on Human Rights.

6. Specifically there is concern about how effective the Council's rights monitoring will be, with NGOs expressing worries at continuing infractions, eg the fourth regular council session closed in Geneva in 2006 having:
   - failed to criticise the Sudanese government for involvement in the Darfur disaster;
   - agreed only on further reporting on Darfur, with no effective action;
   - failed to address urgent issues in Burma, Iran, Sri Lanka, and Uzbekistan.

3.2.2 UN High Commissioner for Human Rights

1. The UNHCHR is the official who heads the UN's human rights efforts, under the leadership of the Secretary-General and subject to the mandates given to him or her by the General Assembly, ECOSOC and the Council.

2. Appointment is by the Secretary-General subject to approval by the General Assembly, with a four-year term, the possibility of one renewal, and subject to geographical rotation.

3. The position was established in 1993 following the Vienna World Conference on Human Rights, despite a lack of enthusiasm of the then Secretary General Boutros-Ghali, although subsequently Secretary-General Kofi Annan was more sympathetic to human rights concerns.

4. The responsibilities of the UNHCHR include:
   - promotion and protection of effective enjoyment of civil, cultural, economic, political, and social and developmental rights;
   - provision of advisory and technical services, and financial assistance, to states requesting them;
   - co-ordination of the UN human rights education and public information programmes;
   - playing an active role in the removal of obstacles to the full realisation of human rights;
   - establishing field presences in sensitive areas from Burundi, Cambodia and Colombia to Guatemala, Mongolia and Togo.

5. The office has been held as follows:
   - 1994–7 Jose Ayala-Lasso, former Ecuadorean foreign minister;
   - 1997–2002 Mary Robinson, former President of Ireland;
   - 2002–3 Sergio Vieira de Mello, former Brazilian and UN diplomat, killed by a bomb in Baghdad;
   - 2004 Louise Arbour, former Canadian Supreme Court Justice.

3.2.3 Other UN organs with human right involvement

General Assembly (GA)

1. Chapter IV, Article 13, provides that the GA shall initiate studies and make recommendations under paragraph:

(a) for promoting international political cooperation and development of international law; and

(b) for promoting international cooperation in the economic, social, cultural, educational and health fields, and assisting in the realisation of human rights and fundamental freedoms for all without distinction as to race, sex, language or religion.

2. The GA usually votes by simple majority and all members are treated equally, having one vote regardless of size or population.

3. Most business is conducted on a consensus basis without necessarily taking votes, although certain matters require a two-thirds majority such as:
   • accession of new members;
   • matters of peace and security;
   • budgetary concerns.

4. The GA is empowered under Article 10 to discuss any matters within the scope of the Charter, although the only reference to human rights in the Charter is in Article 13.

5. There is no provision for the GA to decide for itself the extent to which it would promote human rights issues, and historically this led to arguments by and disagreements with individual states, eg South Africa when the UN condemned apartheid.

6. Nowadays with the operation of the Council and the supervision of the UNHCHR responsibilities are clearer, although states still object when criticised for alleged human rights abuses.

Security Council (SC)

1. The SC paid little attention to human rights during the Cold War, but did eventually condemn apartheid, originally raised as an issue by India in 1946.

2. The UN response was the Westphalian attitude that South African citizens of Indian origin were no one else's business.

3. The SC only imposed a mandatory arms embargo on South Africa under Chapter VII in 1977, followed by rejection in 1984 of the white-imposed new constitution.
4. However, over the years the idea of what constitutes threats to peace gradually expanded and there developed an indirect approach to protecting human rights.
5. With the ending of colonialism the SC often disagreed about human rights issues with other states represented through the General Assembly.
6. The Security Council has 15 members, ten of which rotate, but is effectively controlled by the five powers who have the veto, ie:
   • Britain;
   • France;
   • China;
   • Soviet Union (now Russia);
   • United States.
7. The future of the UK's SC seat and veto is unclear in the context of the revised proposals for the EU 'constitution' and it may be that the UK will at some point be substituted on the SC by the EU.
8. The Security Council can often stymie human rights by use of the veto, eg the US invariably protects Israel whatever its policy towards the Palestinians and despite breaches of human rights by both sides.
9. The Cold War inhibited other actions, now apparent from the increase in post-Cold War UN authorisation of military force since 1990, eg:
   • Iraq;
   • Somalia;
   • former Yugoslavia;
   • Rwanda;
   • Haiti.
10. Other important developments have included:
   • sanctioning peace-keeping operations;
   • establishing the former Yugoslavia and Rwanda genocide tribunals.

11. Another significant trend is that conflicts now mostly occur within, rather than between, states.

3.3 The Covenants

1. The covenants continue the process of creating the International Bill of Human Rights, starting with the UN Charter in 1945 and the 1948 Universal Declaration, but not concluded in the immediate post-war period because of acute and growing post-war tensions between the Soviet Bloc and the West.

2. These covenants are in fact protocols that reflect different basic rights objectives:
   - the (first) Optional Protocol was the ICCPR 1966, generally more amenable to Western states and providing emphasis on individual civil and political rights and freedoms;
   - this was reinforced by the (second) Optional Protocol in 1990, whose objective was to aim towards abolition of the death penalty;
   - in contrast the ICESR 1966 tended to be preferred by Eastern bloc states, concentrating on collective economic and social rights.

3. The language used in the protocols also reflects this as the:
   - ICCPR used more immediate and in places absolute terms in respect of its objectives;
   - ICESCR reflected hopes of progressive realisation dependent on eventual availability of resources.

4. The development into the International Bill of Rights was reinforced by the inter-dependence of the UDHR and the 1966 Protocols, the:
   - former from UDHR Articles 1-22;
   - latter from UDHR Articles 23-28.

5. There were also other equivalencies or cross links between the 1966 covenants themselves that gave coherency to the combined International Bill eg:

- ICCPR Article 18: parental right to choose a child's education compared with ICESCR Article 13: child's right to education and parental right to choose schools;
- ICCPR Article 22: right to freedom of association compared with ICESCR Article 8: right to be a member of a trade union.
6. They were dealt with separately partly because of Cold War differences and ideological confrontation plus other reasons recognised during the drafting stage including:
- large-scale decolonisation immediately post war and in the 1950s;
- changing balances of diplomatic and military strength during that period;
- the difficult reality of turning aspirational UDHR notions into more widely acceptable binding legal obligations.

3.3.1 ICCPR

The ICCPR contains 51 articles and two optional Protocols.

Part I
1. Contains the first article stating that all people have the right of self-determination and are entitled freely to:
- determine their political status;
- pursue their economic, social and cultural development.
2. All peoples (plural) are able freely to dispose of their natural wealth and resources for their mutual benefit, regardless of international economic obligations to cooperate, and under no circumstances should a people be deprived of its own means of subsistence.
3. Self-determination is to be promoted by states and those responsible for non-self governing territories.
4. Article 1 does *not* explain how one determines what is meant by peoples, or a people.

Part II

Contains Articles 2–5, dealing with:

1. Respect within states for all individuals for the covenant rights without distinction of any kind whether race, colour, sex, language, religion, political or other opinion, national or social origin, property, birth or other status.

2. Adoption by states of the machinery necessary to implement this.

3. The need for states parties to ensure the equal right of men and women to enjoy the civil and political rights contained in the covenant.

4. Limited derogation is allowed in times of public emergency, but nothing in the covenant is to be interpreted as working against the grain of the document.

Part III

Contains Articles 6–27, the heart of the covenant, dealing with:

1. Inherent right to life, freedom from torture, inhuman or degrading treatment, and from slavery, servitude and the slave trade.

2. The right to liberty and security of person, without arbitrary arrest or detention, and humane treatment when deprived of liberty.

3. No imprisonment on civil (ie non-criminal) matters eg for debt.

4. Freedom of movement and residence within a territory, and no expulsion from a territory without compelling reason, eg national security.

5. Equality before courts and tribunals with fair trials, no retrospective criminal laws, and right of recognition for everyone before the law.

6. No arbitrary or unlawful interference with privacy, family, home or correspondence, freedom of thought, conscience and religion, and the right for everybody to hold opinions without interference.

7. Prohibition of propaganda for war and advocacy of

national, racial or religious hatred and incitement to discrimination, hostility or violence.

8. Rights of peaceful assembly and freedom of association, and recognition that the family is the natural and fundamental group unit of society with the right to marry freely.

9. Protection of children without discrimination, and the right to take part in public affairs.

10. Equality before the law, and protection of ethnic, religious and linguistic minorities.

Part IV

1. Article 28 establishes a Human Rights Committee, the remainder of the ICCPR dealing with consequential organisational and administrative arrangements.

2. The first optional Protocol authorises the Human Rights Committee established under Article 28 to receive and consider communications from individuals claiming to be victims of a violation by a state party.

3. The second optional Protocol abolishes the death sentence for ratifying states parties.

3.3.2 ICESCR

Part I

Article 1 is the only article in Part I and is the same as that in the ICCPR.

Part II

Articles 2–5 contain undertakings to take steps, especially economic and technical but within available resources to guarantee the rights contained in the ICESCR without discrimination, with a proviso for developing countries that they can limit the extent of their commitment to economic rights:

- the states parties undertake to ensure equality between the sexes in respect of economic, social and cultural rights;

- these rights are expressed in terms of resource-constrained objectives, rather than absolute obligations.

Part III

Contains Articles 6–15, the main substantive provisions, dealing with:

1. Rights to work in just and favourable conditions, to form and join trades union, and to have social security and insurance.
2. Recognition of the family, especially children and young persons.
3. The need for an adequate standard of living including food, clothing, housing and continuous improvement of living conditions.
4. Achieving the highest attainable standard of physical and mental health.
5. Provision of compulsory and free primary education, and education for all to develop fully the human personality and sense of dignity.
6. Allowing broad cultural enjoyment, including the benefits of scientific progress and its applications, and literary and artistic productions.

Part IV

Deals with submission of reports by states parties, and consequential administrative procedures.

3.4 UN Conventions

3.4.1 UN and international law rights structure

1. The UN rights structure is based on the 1945 UN Charter, Article 103 of which says that in the event of a conflict between Members of the UN under the Charter and their obligations under any other international agreement, Charter obligations shall prevail.
2. The International Bill of (Human) Rights then combines the 1948 Universal Declaration with the two 1966

covenants or protocols (ICCPR and ICESCR) that entered into force in 1977, together with the 1990 second protocol dealing with abolition of the death penalty, which read together have similar status to other Conventions discussed below.

3. *'Jus cogens'* are principles or peremptory norms of international law so fundamental that no state can ignore them or attempt to contract out of them by treaty or in any other way, and construction of all international law has to take this into account (see 3.5).

4. Article 53 of the Vienna Convention on the Law of Treaties 1969 says that any treaty conflicting with this is void and examples of *jus cogens* include:
   - genocide;
   - slave trading;
   - prohibition of apartheid.

5. The rest of this section sets out the basics of some of the most important UN Conventions.

3.4.2 Convention on the Prevention and Punishment of the Crime of Genocide 1951

1. Many states were guilty of genocide during the twentieth century, including the USSR, China, Germany, Cambodia, Japan and Rwanda.

2. Although what is now called genocide has been perpetrated throughout history, the word itself was coined during the Second World War by the Polish scholar Raphael Lemkin.

3. Genocide comprises two essential elements:
   a) mental, ie intent to destroy, in whole or in part, a national, ethnical, racial or religious group, as such;
   b) physical, comprising one or more of the following five acts:
      - killing group members;
      - causing serious mental or bodily harm to group members, eg rape or mutilation;
      - deliberately inflicting on group members conditions

of life calculated to bring about its physical destruction in whole or in part, eg deprivation of physical resources such as water, blockading food or detention;
- imposing measures intended to prevent births within the group, eg forcible sterilisation or abortion;
- forcibly transferring children of the group to another group.

4. In addition to genocide there can also be, even prior to killing:
- conspiracy to commit genocide;
- direct and public incitement to commit genocide;
- attempt to commit genocide;
- complicity in genocide.

5. 140 states are parties to the Convention, but some major states such as Indonesia, Japan and Nigeria are not.

3.4.3 The Convention on the Elimination of all Forms of Racial Discrimination 1966

1. This is divided into three parts containing 25 articles with Article 1 defining racial discrimination as any distinction, exclusion, restriction or preference based on race, colour, descent, or national or ethnic origin which nullifies or impairs equal recognition, enjoyment or exercise of political, economic, social or cultural human rights and fundamental freedoms.

2. This Convention was enthusiastically embraced by states keen to demonstrate their eagerness to condemn racial discrimination in the context of post-war decolonisation.

3. It particularly condemns racial segregation, apartheid and propaganda, and in Article 5 guarantees a wide range of rights including:
- equal treatment before tribunals;
- security of person and participation in elections;
- freedom of movement and nationality;
- marriage and choice of spouse;
- property and inheritance;

- freedom of thought, conscience and religion, opinion and expression;
- freedom of assembly and association;
- economic, social and cultural rights;
- work and trades union rights;
- housing, health, education and cultural activities.

4. 173 states are parties to this Convention, although many states have made reservations.

3.4.4 Convention on the Elimination of All Forms of Discrimination Against Women 1981 (CEDAW)

1. This Convention:
   a) was adopted by the General Assembly in 1979;
   b) is sometimes regarded as an international bill of rights for women.

2. It comprises a preamble and 30 articles and after defining discrimination in this context, it establishes a national agenda for ending it.

3. Discrimination against women is any distinction, exclusion or restriction made on the basis of sex which has the effect or purpose of impairing or nullifying the recognition, enjoyment or exercise by women of human rights and fundamental freedoms in the political, economic, social, cultural, civil or any other field.

4. By ratifying the Convention, states accept a number of basic tenets, including:
- incorporation of sexual equality principles into domestic law;
- abolition of discriminatory laws and adoption of suitable ones;
- elimination of discriminatory acts against women by individuals or organisations;
- establishment of tribunals to protect women;
- the principle that equality should apply in political and public life, health, education and employment;
- affirmation of women's rights to bear children and to

acquire and change nationality for themselves and their children.

5. The Convention has 185 states parties, over 95% of the members of the UN.

3.4.5 Convention Against Torture and Other Cruel, Inhuman and Degrading Treatment or Punishment 1987

1. Entered into force in June 1987 with three parts and 33 articles, the background referred to in the Preamble being:
   - UN Charter Article 55;
   - UDHR Article 5;
   - ICCPR Article 7;
   - Declaration on the Protection of All Persons from Being Subjected to Torture and Other Cruel, Inhuman or Degrading Treatment or Punishment adopted by the General Assembly December 1975.

2. Article 1 defines torture as:
   - any act by which severe pain or suffering, whether physical or mental, is intentionally inflicted on a person for such purposes as obtaining from him or a third person information or a confession; or
   - punishing him for an act he or a third person has committed or is suspected of having committed; or
   - intimidating or coercing him or a third person;
   - when such pain or suffering is inflicted by or at the instigation of or with the consent or acquiescence of a public official or other person acting in an official capacity;
   - but not including pain or suffering arising only from, or inherent in or incidental to lawful sanctions.

3. Under Article 2 no exceptional circumstances whatsoever may be invoked to justify torture, and *refoulement* (sending or extraditing to a state where torture is likely to occur) is forbidden by Article 3.

4. Other important provisions are that states must:
   * make torture a domestic extraditable crime and arrest suspects;
   * keep interrogation methods, practices and rules under review;
   * investigate suspicious circumstances.
5. Part II establishes a Committee against Torture comprising ten independent experts to serve four-year terms.
6. States parties must submit reports to the UN through the Secretary General indicating measures taken to fulfil their obligations under the Convention.
7. The Convention has 144 states parties.

3.4.6 Convention on the Rights of the Child 1989

1. This is divided into three parts, Part I, Articles 1–41 *inter alia* dealing with the following matters:
   * defining a child as every human being under 18 years, unless majority is attained earlier;
   * stating that in all actions the interests of the child must be the primary consideration;
   * children's inherent rights to life, a name, nationality, identity, and to live with their parents;
   * states must prevent illicit transfer and non-return of children;
   * due weight must be given to children's wishes with respect for their rights to freedom of thought, conscience, religion, association and assembly;
   * there must be no interference with privacy, family, home or correspondence and access to information, and recognition of parents' common responsibilities;
   * there should be protection of children from physical or mental violence, injury or abuse, neglect or negligent mistreatment, maltreatment, exploitation or sexual abuse;
   * further articles deal with adoption, refugees, disabilities, health, care proceedings, education and cultural rights,

and the right not to be exploited.

2. The Convention has 193 states parties.

3. There are two optional protocols to this Convention, both dated 2000:
   - one is designed to ensure that states parties take all feasible measures to ensure that minors under the age of 18 years shall not be compulsorily recruited into their armed forces nor take a direct part in hostilities;
   - the other prohibits sale of children, child prostitution, child pornography and other activities such as transfer of children's organs for profit and engagement of children in forced labour.

3.4.7 Migrant Workers Convention 1990

1. The International Convention on the Protection of the Rights of All Migrant Workers and Members of Their Families entered into force on 1 July 2003, with 37 states parties.

2. It is in nine parts:
   I   Scope and definitions (Articles 1-6);
   II   Non-discrimination with respect to rights (Article 7);
   III   Human rights of all migrant workers and members of their families (Articles 8-35);
   IV   Other rights of documented workers and families (Articles 36-56);
   V   Particular category provisions (Articles 57-63);
   VI   Humane conditions for international migration of workers and families (Articles 64-71);
   VII   Application of the Convention (Articles 72-78);
   VIII   General conditions (Articles 79-84);
   IX   Final conditions (Articles 85-93).

3. The primary objective is to protect migrant workers and their families because of their particular vulnerability to human rights breaches.

4. The main distinction is between Parts 3 and 4, with Part 3 applying to all migrant workers but Part 4 only to

authorised or documented workers in a regular situation.
5. This Convention was needed because even when implementing other UN Conventions many states specifically excluded undocumented migrant workers thus disenfranchising them from human rights protection.

3.4.8 UN Disabilities Convention

1. The Convention on the Rights of Persons with Disabilities and its Optional Protocol opened for signature on 30 March 2007 with:
   - 100 signatories to the Convention;
   - 55 signatories to the Optional Protocol;
   - one ratification (Jamaica).
2. The Convention has 50 articles and the Optional Protocol.
3. The purpose of the Convention is to promote, protect and ensure the full and equal enjoyment of all human rights and fundamental freedoms by all persons with disabilities, and to promote respect for their inherent dignity.
4. The definition of persons with disability include those who have long-term physical, mental, intellectual or sensory impairments which in interaction with various barriers may hinder their full and effective participation in society on an equal basis with others.
5. States parties to the Optional Protocol recognise the competence of the Committee on the Rights of Persons with Disabilities and the Committee's function is to receive and consider communications from individuals or groups claiming to be victims of state violations of the Convention.

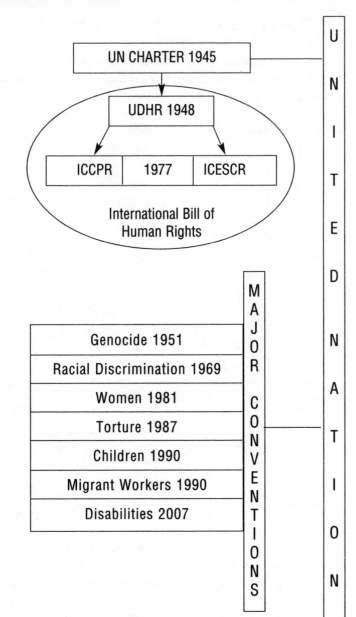

3.5 *Jus cogens*

1. Although the scope of this book excludes public international law a brief summary of some basic definitions is desirable, as they widely resonate in global human rights, and this section refers exclusively to public and not private international law:
   - public international law is the law of nations under which states are regarded as individual members of a common polity, bound by a common rule of agreement or custom, as opposed to municipal (state internal) law, ie the rules that bind local (ie national) jurisdictions;
   - private international law or conflict of laws deals with private individuals' disputes (including legal persons ie corporations) where different legal jurisdictions are involved eg a trading dispute between a French and an Indian company, or a divorce involving different nationalities and legal systems.
2. Recognised sources of public international law under Article 38 of the Statute of the International Court of Justice are:
   - treaties (rather like contracts made between governments);
   - custom (a bit like international common law or widely accepted rules);
   - general principles of law (a means or mechanism to address international issues not already subject to customary rules or treaty).
3. International law operates according to various norms which are concerned with how rights work and sometimes overriding principles are recognised:
   - *'erga omnes'* is Latin for in relation or referring to everyone, and in the international law context it is used as a legal term to describe obligations owed by states to the rest of the world;
   - *'jus cogens'* are principles of international law so fundamental that no state is able to ignore them or contract out of them by treaty.

4. Examples illustrating these norms that cannot be breached are:
- piracy;
- slave trading;
- genocide;
- racial discrimination.

Being involved in such activities is or should be repugnant to the whole of mankind.

CHAPTER 4

Regional Regimes

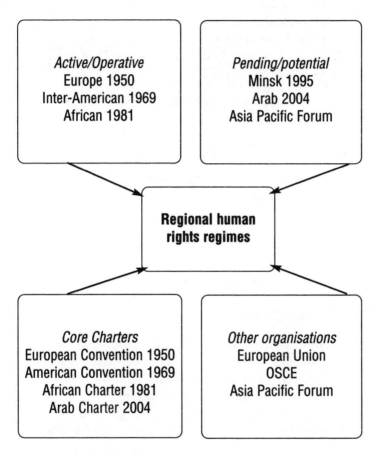

Active/Operative
Europe 1950
Inter-American 1969
African 1981

Pending/potential
Minsk 1995
Arab 2004
Asia Pacific Forum

Regional human rights regimes

Core Charters
European Convention 1950
American Convention 1969
African Charter 1981
Arab Charter 2004

Other organisations
European Union
OSCE
Asia Pacific Forum

4.1 The regimes

4.1.1 Active operative regional systems

Contrasting with the universal or global system, there are three regional structures, in descending order of development, effectiveness and sophistication:

- European (1950);
- Inter-American (1969);
- African (1981).

4.1.2 Pending/potential systems

There are other systems not properly effective, yet with potential:
- Commonwealth of Independent States Convention on Human Rights (Minsk) 1995;
- Arab Charter on Human Rights 2004;
- Asia Pacific Forum.

4.1.3 Other organisations

Other organisations play some role in regional and inter-regional human rights affairs, depending on how human rights are defined:
- European Union (EU);
- the Organisation for Security and Cooperation in Europe (OSCE);
- Asia Pacific Forum.

4.1.4 Core charters

This chapter concentrates (although not exclusively) on Europe, the Americas and Africa, whose core charters are the:
- European Convention on Human Rights 1950 (an instrument of the Council of Europe);
- American Convention on Human Rights 1969;
- African Charter of Human and People's Rights 1981.

4.2 Europe

As this book has three chapters devoted to human rights issues specifically in the UK and Europe, more detail is given here about other regional regimes, although in reality Europe has the most advanced regional system when the scope, influence and effectiveness of its operations are considered.

4.2.1 Principal documents

Within Europe, the main charters and conventions are as follows (and care should be taken not to confuse regional conventions with those of the UN):

- Convention for the Protection of Human Rights and Fundamental Freedoms 1950 together with a number of Protocols extending its provisions (ECHR);
- European Social Charter 1961 with Protocols, revised 1996;
- European Convention for the Prevention of Torture and Inhuman or Degrading Treatment or Punishment 1987;
- European Charter for Regional or Minority Languages 1992;
- Convention on Human Rights and Biomedicine 1997;
- Charter of Fundamental Rights of the European Union 2000.

4.2.2 Convention rights

1. The ECHR ('the Convention') came into existence as a result of the establishment of the Council of Europe in 1949, for a number of reasons:
   - reaction to Second World War atrocities and determination to avoid repetition;
   - to encourage cooperation rather than conflict between European and neighbouring states;
   - to avoid the dangers that arose from the punishment and humiliation inflicted on Germany after the First World War;
   - to establish an effective and enforceable regional agenda, based on the new global regime.
2. Care must be taken not to confuse the Council of Europe with the EU.
3. The terms were similar to early drafts of the UN Covenant on Civil and Political Rights, but contained no provisions on self-determination or minority group rights.

4. To ensure effective implementation, Article 1 requires the parties to secure convention rights to everyone within their jurisdiction.

5. Article 13 requires states to provide an effective remedy before a national authority for everyone whose rights have been violated.

6. Subsequent Protocols were needed to implement provisions that could not be agreed in 1950, including rights relating to:
   - property;
   - education;
   - free elections;
   - movement and residence;
   - abolition of the death penalty.

7. All 47 states which are members of the Council of Europe are parties to the Convention, whose broad emphasis has tended towards rectifying delay in process and promoting rights of non-interference, compared with concerns about tackling systematic violence and forced disappearances in Latin America.

4.2.3 European Social Charter

1. The emphasis immediately after the Second World War was on civil and political rights and the need to foster and guarantee democracy, so economic and social rights were subsequently recognised in the European Social Charter.

2. There are various Protocols, but the system was updated in 1996 by a revised and consolidated charter.

3. This has led to more fragmentation than is the case for the Convention, which all 47 Council of Europe members have ratified.

4. In the case of the Social Charter, 17 members have not ratified any of its provisions or Protocols.

5. The Charter includes employment conditions covering:
   - non-discrimination;
   - prohibition of forced labour;

- trades union rights and decent working conditions;
- equal pay;
- prohibition of child labour;
- maternity protection.
6. Additionally 'social cohesion' conditions cover:
   - health protection and social security;
   - rights relating to families, children and the elderly;
   - migrant workers.

4.3 The Americas

4.3.1 Principal documents

There are a number of important documents to consider here:
1. American Declaration of the Rights and Duties of Man 1948.
2. American Convention on Human Rights 1969 (see below), together with the:
   - Additional Protocol to the American Convention on Human Rights in the Area of Economic, Social and Cultural Rights 1988;
   - Protocol to the American Convention on Human Rights to Abolish the Death Penalty 1990.
3. Specific conventions:
   - Inter-American Convention to Prevent and Punish Torture 1985;
   - Inter-American Convention on the Forced Disappearance of Persons 1994;
   - Inter-American Convention on the Prevention, Punishment and Eradication of Violence against Women 1994.

4.3.2 The OAS apparatus

1. The Organisation of American States (OAS) originated in the International Union of American Republics of 1890, but was established in its modern form at the 1948 Bogota conference.

2. The 1948 Charter entered into force in 1951, and was subsequently amended by the Protocols of:
   - Buenos Aires 1967;
   - Cartagena de Indias 1985;
   - Washington 1992;
   - Managua 1993.
3. It has a number of objectives, including:
   - strengthening peace and security on the continent;
   - promoting democracy;
   - providing for common action against aggression;
   - seeking solutions to political, juridical and economic problems.
4. It operates through General Assembly annual meetings, consultation between foreign ministers, and has a General Secretariat and Permanent Council located in Washington DC.
5. The Inter-American Commission on Human Rights was created in 1959, leading to the Convention in 1969, which entered into force in 1978.
6. The Latin and South America political climate has been very different from that of Europe, with unelected military governments being the norm until recent years so there has been more concern than in Europe over torture, disappearances and corrupt judiciary.
7. OAS membership:
   - 35 members;
   - 25 ratifications of Convention;
   - 20 recognise Court's jurisdiction;
   - Cuba is suspended.

4.3.3 American Declaration of the Rights and Duties of Man 1948

1. This pre-dates the UN Universal Declaration and European Convention, but did not in itself establish the American regime and supervisory apparatus; its content is similar to the Universal Declaration, including economic and social rights.

2. There are also ten articles setting out the responsibilities and duties of the citizen, eg to:
   • obtain education for himself and his children;
   • vote;
   • render civil and military service to his country.

4.3.4 American Convention on Human Rights 1969

1. This is the treaty based on the above declaration and sometimes referred to as the Pact of San Jose, Costa Rica. It:
   • followed the Third Special Inter-American Conference in Buenos Aires in 1967;
   • approved the incorporation into the Charter of the Organisation's broad standards for economic, social and educational rights, thus differing from European arrangements.
2. Additionally, there are specific articles covering the right to:
   • juridical personality (Article 3);
   • a name (Article 18);
   • nationality (Article 20).
3. There is also a right of reply (Article 14), and rights of the child (Article 19).
4. The American Convention contains specific rights to:
   • property, incorporated in Article 21 rather than by Protocol;
   • freedom of movement and residence (Article 22);
   • participate in government (Article 23);
   • equal protection of the law (Article 24);
   • judicial protection by the laws (Article 25).
5. Chapter III contains only one article (26) whereby states undertake to adopt internal and international progressive measures to achieve the full realisation of the rights implicit in the economic, social, educational, scientific and cultural standards of the OAS Charter.
6. The additional 1988 Protocol introduced obligations relating to:

- non-discrimination (Article 3);
- the right to work and to have just, equitable and satisfactory conditions of work with trade union rights (Articles 6, 7 and 8);
- further rights to social security and health in Articles 9 and 10;
- a healthy environment by Article 11.

7. These supplementary provisions also included:
   - food and education (Articles 12 and 13);
   - the benefits of culture under Article 14;
   - protection of the family, children, elderly and handicapped (Articles 15, 16, 17 and 18 respectively).

8. The 1990 Protocol addresses abolition of the death penalty; if and when adopted and ratified by American states it will not under Article 2 allow any reservations, but would not extend to war-time or extremely serious crimes of a military nature.

4.3.5 Inter-American Convention on the Forced Disappearance of Persons (1994)

1. Forced disappearance abuses of human rights were endemic in Latin and South America for much of the twentieth century, so this treaty was essential.

2. The Preamble said that OAS members were:
   - disturbed by the persistence of the forced disappearance of persons which affronted the conscience of the hemisphere;
   - concerned at violations of numerous non-derogable and essential human rights in the American and UN Declarations and in the American Convention.

3. They undertook not to practise or tolerate forced disappearances, defined in Article II as having four essential elements:
   - depriving persons of their freedom in whatever way;
   - perpetration by or with the support of the state;
   - absence of information and refusal to acknowledge occurrences;

- impedance or negation of legal and procedural remedies.
4. Forced disappearances could not be treated as political offences and criminal prosecutions would not be subject to statutes of limitation ie they could be prosecuted at any time in the future with no defence of superior orders.
5. War, threats of political instability, or other public emergencies, would not justify the crime and:
   - detainees should be held in an officially recognised establishment;
   - they should be brought before properly constituted judicial authority without delay;
   - states must provide mutual assistance to search for, trace and identify victims.

4.3.6 Comparisons

1. The American regime is more complex than the European system being based on the Declaration and Convention.
2. It is more ambitious than the European Convention because the Inter-American Commission:
   - hears cases;
   - makes visits;
   - prepares country reports on the human rights position of Member States.
3. Stemming from different continental political histories violations in Europe tend to be individual rather than collective, often because of procedural incompetence eg delay in providing hearings and solutions, whereas in the Americas there have been repeated and large-scale gross violations.
4. There is no enforcement procedure in the Americas and decisions are not necessarily accepted as legally binding, although there is a 'follow-up' mechanism; in Europe the Committee of Ministers guarantees remedial action.

4.4 Africa

4.4.1 Principal documents

The main African documents are the:
1. 1981 African Charter, containing 68 articles, divided into Rights and Duties, Measures of Safeguard, and General Provisions;
2. 1998 Protocol on the Establishment of an African Court on Human and People's Rights containing 35 articles;
3. OAU Convention Governing the Specific Aspects of Refugee Problems in Africa 1969, with 15 articles and concerned with refugees, asylum, prohibition of subversion, non-discrimination and connected matters in the African context;
4. African Charter on the Rights and Welfare of the Child 1990 dealing with freedoms, education, protection against abuse, responsibilities and organisational matters.

4.4.2 The OAU apparatus

1. The Organisation of African Unity (OAU) was until recently the regional body of the African states, having 53 states parties, the Charter of the OAU being adopted in 1963.
2. In 1981 the Assembly of Heads of States and Government of the OAU adopted the African Charter on Human and People's Rights, coming into force in 1986.
3. There was only one implementation instrument, the Commission, with no enforcement provisions ie it operated only as an advisory body so its scope was more limited than in Europe or the Americas.
4. The emphasis was on inviolability of borders and one of the main African characteristics has been reluctance to promote human rights or take effective action when violations occurred.

5. The First OAU Ministerial Conference on Human Rights met in April 1999 in Mauritius, issuing an impressive Declaration and Plan of Action, but in 2002 it was disbanded and a new African Union (AU) organisation was launched in Durban, South Africa, to replace the OAU.
6. The OAU Charter did not deal with human rights although they are now mentioned in the AU Charter.
7. Critics claim that in 39 years of existence the OAU did little to protect the human rights of African citizens; it remains to be seen whether the AU can do better, considering the pandemic continental problems.

4.4.3 The African Union

The AU structure is broadly modelled on the EU, so is not primarily a human rights organisation although possessing some human rights machinery, the organisation comprising the:
1. Assembly, made up of members' heads of state with functions including common policies, membership, and conflict resolution;
2. Executive Council, ie the foreign ministers of its members whose functions include foreign trade, social security, food, agriculture and communications;
3. Permanent Representative Committee, consisting of the Ambassadors to the AU whose function is to prepare the work for the Executive Council;
4. Commission (Secretariat), Specialised Technical Committees, Pan-African Parliament, Economic, Social and Cultural Council, and three Financial Institutions.

4.4.4 AU Human Rights bodies

The AU bodies possessing a human rights focus are the:
1. African Court on Human and People's Rights, established in 2005 and integrating with the African Court of Justice, to overcome the limitations of the Commission by complementing and extending its mandate.

2. Peace and Security Council, with 15 members responsible for monitoring and intervening in conflicts, to be advised by a Council of Elders with an African force at its disposal.

The Court

1. The election of judges for the combined court took place in January 2006 at the mid-term AU summit and judges were sworn into office in July 2006.

2. Three administrative sessions were held later in 2006 to establish Rules of Procedure, structural issues and budgetary matters.

3. The AU has been requested to pursue, intensify and increase its support for the new court and its 11 judges so this initiative is very much work in progress for African human rights.

The Peace and Security Council

1. The first practical steps towards the council were taken in February 2004 in Libya with agreement to establish a 15,000-strong peace-keeping force divided into five regional brigades, the 'African Standby Force', but it is likely to comprise existing military units of individual states ear-marked for action as required.

2. It is roughly modelled on the UN version, but without power to decide independently on military or humanitarian intervention, although it may be allowed to commence 'peace support operations' and send observers to trouble spots.

3. The Libyan leader Moammar Gadaffi's radical idea that there should be a pan-African army was rejected by other AU leaders.

4. The EU has pledged about $US300 million towards it but African contributions are already problematical.

5. The Peace and Security Council held in 2007 frequent meetings on a variety of problem areas such as Darfur, Somalia, Cote D'Ivoire and this too is work in progress for African and world human rights.

6. So far the Council has failed to halt extensive rights violations in Darfur, prevented from effective deployment by meager resources and obstruction by the Sudanese government.

4.5 The Minsk Convention

1. The Commonwealth of Independent States Convention on Human Rights (Minsk) 1995 was:
   - opened for signature in May 1995;
   - originally signed by Armenia, Belarus, Kyrgyzstan, Moldova, Russia and Tajikistan;
   - subsequently ratified by the Russian Federation, Tajikistan and Georgia Belarus;
   - entered into force in August 1998.
2. The control mechanism comprises the CIS Commission on Human Rights which monitors practice by issuing recommendations, the members of the Commission being appointed representatives of the states parties.
3. The CIS Convention does not offer as extensive protection as the ECHR and the Council of Europe is concerned that difficulties might arise for states such as Russia, which are now subject to both Conventions.
4. Particular worries arose about the submission of individual applications to the European Court of Human Rights as the Council of Europe believes that the CIS Commission cannot offer equivalent protection to the European Court, nor are its recommendations enforceable.
5. Some states subject to the CIS Convention cannot aspire to membership of the Council of Europe, so they at least have some regional safeguards in place, albeit less satisfactory than for Europe.

4.6 Arab Declaration and Charter

4.6.1 The Cairo Declaration on Human Rights in Islam 1990

1. This was the Arab world's precursor to their Charter, reinforcing the UN documents and issued following a conference in Cairo in 1990.
2. The Declaration contains the Preamble and 25 articles and is issued to serve as general guidance for Member States in the field of human rights following a report of legal experts.
3. It is expressed in Islamic religious terms, referring to the human family descended from Adam, subordinate to Allah, with life being a God-given gift.
4. It addresses a variety of rights which as well as the family include:
   - humanitarian concerns;
   - sexual equality;
   - prohibition of colonialism;
   - freedom of work and movement;
   - ownership of physical and intellectual property;
   - security, equality and freedom from hostage taking.
5. It concludes by asserting that:
   - authority is a trust;
   - abuse or malicious exploitation thereof is prohibited;
   - all rights and freedoms stipulated in the Declaration are subject to the Islamic Shar'ia, the only source of reference for explanation or clarification of any of its articles.

4.6.2 Arab Charter on Human Rights

1. The Arab Charter on Human Rights 1994 was a Charter of the Council of the League of Arab States, whose basic precepts as indicated in the Preamble were to:
   - refer to the Arab world as the birthplace of civilisation and cradle of religions;

- reject racism and Zionism;
- acknowledge the eternal principles of brotherhood established by the Islamic Shar'ia and other divinely-revealed religions;
- express belief in the rule of law;
- reaffirm the principles of the UN Charter and the International Bill of Human Rights together with the Cairo Declaration on Human Rights in Islam 1990.

2. The 1994 Charter did not come into force due to an insufficient number of ratifications, but a new Draft Charter was adopted in 2004, modernised by bringing it into compliance with current international human rights standards.

3. This text was adopted by the Arab Standing Committee for Human Rights 5-14 January 2004 and contains 53 articles, the first of which seeks to place human rights at the centre of the key national concerns of Arab states, with (*inter alia*) articles providing:

- self-determination with control of national wealth and resources;
- enjoyment of rights without regard to discrimination, whether based on race, colour, sex, language, religious belief, opinion, thought, national or social origin, wealth, birth or physical or mental disability (very wide in aspiration);
- right to life and protection against arbitrary deprivation of life;
- allowance of death penalty for most serious crimes but not for individuals under the age of 19 years;
- no physical or psychological torture or cruel, inhuman, degrading or humiliating treatment;
- many other rights and protections including no medical or scientific experimentation on people without consent and no slavery, but with rights to fair trial and liberty of the person.

4. The approach seems to be to take the basic UN International Bill of Human Rights, place it in the context

of the Cairo Declaration on Human Rights in Islam, reject racialism and Zionism, and then add specific categories of rights.

5. It is difficult to compare this Charter with better known UN or European ones because it contains both subtle and overt differences and is untried in practice, but some points can be noted eg:

   - Article 7 says that sentence of death shall not be imposed on persons under 19 years of age, unless otherwise stipulated in the laws in force at the time of the commission of the crime, the effect being to perpetuate the possibility both of capital punishment and application to minors;

   - Article 19 says no one can be tried twice for the same offence and anyone whose innocence is established by a final judgment shall be entitled to compensation for the damage cause; these advantages are not available under English law.

6. As in the African case, whether this is signed, ratified and honoured by the adoption of satisfactory enforcement procedures and machinery by Islamic states remains to be seen.

4.7 Asia-Pacific Forum of National Human Rights Institutions

1. Asia covers such an extensive and diverse part of the globe that there is little in the way of human rights co-operation compared with Europe, the Americas or even Africa.

2. So organisations such as ASEAN (Association of South East Asian Nations) which were formed to promote economic, social and cultural co-operations and to strengthen regional peace, have virtually no human rights focus to their activities.

3. Furtherance of human rights is, however, the purpose of the Asia-Pacific Forum (APF) established in 1996 and whose objectives are to:

- advance human rights throughout the Asia Pacific area via various member organisations;
- facilitate the formation and growth of national human rights institutions by providing:
  - training;
  - networking;
  - resource-sharing.

4. Membership is only partial amongst Asia Pacific states and examples of non-members are:
   - Myanmar;
   - North Korea;
   - Cambodia.

5. But membership does include some states not necessarily at the forefront of human rights activities:
   - Afghanistan;
   - Nepal;
   - Mongolia.

6. Associate members include:
   - Jordan;
   - Palestine;
   - Qatar.

7. An Advisory Council of Jurists (AJC) was established in 1998 comprising an eminent body of jurists who have held high judicial office, or senior academic or human rights appointments, whose function is to:
   - advise the APF on interpretation and application of international human rights standards;
   - develop regional rights jurisprudence.

8. Issues tackled in recent years include:
   - women's rights (1998);
   - child pornography and the death penalty (1999);
   - trafficking (2001);
   - terrorism and the rule of law (2002);
   - torture, rights to education and internally displaced persons (IDPs) (2005).

9. The 12 annual session was held in Australia in 2007 and principal concerns were the:

- role of national human rights institutions in promoting and protecting the rights of people with disabilities;
- AJC's major report on human rights and the environment.

10. Strategic partnerships have been established with:
- UN Office of the High Commissioner for Human Rights;
- Brookings Institution;
- International Service for Human Rights;
- Raoul Wallenberg Institute;
- Various NGOs and INGOs.

11. Although this does not compare with other regional systems it provides a starting point for a region of huge size, importance, population and diversity to foster and develop human rights, encouraged by states such as Australia and New Zealand which possess developed rights regimes.

12. Apart from this, little progress has been made towards establishing a credible Asian regime, with various reasons being suggested:
- states may regard human rights as an internal matter;
- cultural relativism rejects universalism as an inappropriate Western concept;
- a view that collective security, economic and social interests take precedence over individual rights;
- the size and diversity of the continent.

4.8 The Organisation for Security and Cooperation in Europe (OSCE)

1. The Organisation for Security and Cooperation in Europe (OSCE) asserts a low-profile diplomatic process whose basic purpose is to pre-empt and prevent conflict in three areas:
- human;
- politico-military;
- economic/environmental.

2. It has 55 participating states spanning a geographical area from Vancouver to Vladivostok, so covering four major regions:
   - continental Europe;
   - the Causcasus;
   - Central Asia;
   - North America.
3. Unlike the UN it has no status under international law so its decisions are not legally enforceable but rely on political recognition.
4. The OSCE was launched in Helsinki in 1972, emerging through a series of processes to the Final Act, the 1992 Helsinki Document establishing the basis for the OSCE's Office for Democratic Institutions and Human Rights (ODIHR), located in Poland with a specific human rights mandate to assist participating states to:
   - ensure full respect for human rights and fundamental freedoms;
   - abide by the rule of law;
   - promote principles of democracy and to build, strengthen and protect democratic institutions;
   - promote tolerance throughout society.
5. Functions of the ODIHR include:
   - promotion of democratic elections;
   - providing practical support in consolidating democratic institutions;
   - devising human rights training for governments and civil society;
   - helping participating states to implement international legal obligations and OSCE commitments on terrorism in line with human rights principles;
   - promotion of Roma and Sinti issues.

4.9 The European Union (EU)

4.9.1 Background

1. It is important not to confuse the EU with the Council of Europe's human rights regime, but the EU itself is deeply concerned with human rights issues and claims to be world leader in regional human rights protection.

2. Entry into force of the 1993 Treaty on European Union (TEU) advanced integration of human rights and democratic principles in EU policies, emphasising consolidation of democracy and the rule of law.

3. The 1999 Treaty of Amsterdam inserted a new Article 6 in the TEU reaffirming that:
   - the EU is founded on principles of liberty, democracy, respect for human rights and fundamental freedoms, and the rule of law;
   - serious and persistent violation of those principles would lead to suspension of some state rights under the Union Treaty.

4. The Treaty of Amsterdam incorporated other human rights dimensions including:
   - a clause to combat discrimination;
   - measures concerning asylum, refugees and immigration;
   - provisions relating to employment, working conditions and social protection.

5. The Nice Summit in 2000 proclaimed the EU Charter of Fundamental Rights, codifying materials from various sources including the ECHR, international instruments and common constitutional traditions.

6. The EU fosters human rights in other ways, eg:
   - the Luxembourg Declaration of 1991 and the 1998 Declaration on the fiftieth anniversary of the Universal Declaration;
   - human rights clauses in over 50 bilateral trade and cooperation agreements;
   - funding activities eg assisting the AU.

4.9.2 EU internal human rights

1. Article 6 of the TEU is the basis for demonstrating that internally within the EU human rights are 'general principles' that the EU must respect, stating:
   - Article 6(1): The Union is founded on the principles of liberty, democracy, respect for human rights and fundamental freedoms and the rule of law, principles which are common to the Member States;
   - Article 6(2): The Union shall respect fundamental rights, as guaranteed by the European Convention on Human Rights ... and from the constitutional provisions of Member States, as general principles of Community law;
   - Article 6(4): The Union shall provide itself the means necessary to attain its objectives and carry through its policies.
2. The ECJ is not bound by the ECHR nor by the constitutional provisions of Member States but it is 'guided' and 'inspired' by them and generally should give effect to them under Article 220.
3. There have been unsuccessful proposals for the EU as an entity to accede to the ECHR.
4. The Charter of Fundamental Rights of the EU 2000 guides the Commission on human rights and is the result of a unique procedure designed to set out in a single text the full range of civil, political, economic and social rights of EU citizens and residents.
5. It is divided into six sections addressing:
   - dignity;
   - freedoms;
   - equality;
   - solidarity;
   - citizens' rights;
   - justice.
6. The Charter derives from a variety of sources, the main ones being:

- ECHR;
- Council of Europe's Social Charter;
- Community Charter of Fundamental Social Rights of Workers;
- Other international conventions to which the EU and/or Member States are parties.

7. The legal status is that of a solemn proclamation by the EU's three main institutions, Council, Commission and Parliament, rather than being a binding treaty, and was meant to feed into the proposed European Constitution which was rejected by French and Dutch referenda in 2005.

8. In June 2007 it was agreed by all 27 Member States to try to negotiate a reformed treaty by the end of 2007 for ratification by mid-2009, the objectives being:
   - stronger European leadership;
   - a larger world 'footprint';
   - greater influence for the European and national parliaments;
   - to enable further expansion of the EU, difficult if not impossible without reform.

9. Concerning discrimination under Article 13 of the Treaty of Amsterdam the Council acting unanimously on a proposal from the Commission and after consulting the European Parliament may take appropriate action to combat discrimination based on sex, racial or ethnic origin, religion or belief, disability, age or sexual orientation.

10. The European Union Agency for Fundamental Rights (FRA) was established in 2007 to replace and build on the work of the European Monitoring Centre on Racism and Xenophobia (EUMC).

11. The FRA has three key functions, to:
    - collect information and data;
    - provide advice to the EU and its Member States;
    - promote dialogue with civil society to raise public awareness of fundamental rights.

12. Although politicians and officials express satisfaction with this development, others are sceptical because the FRA will not:
- examine individual complaints;
- have regulatory decision-making powers;
- monitor fundamental rights in the Member States for purposes of Article 7 of the EU Treaty;
- deal with the legality of legislative acts under Article 230 of the Treaty (Court of Justice's power to review legality of Community acts);
- question whether Member States have failed to fulfill obligations under Article 226 of the Treaty (by which the Commission issues a reasoned opinion where it considers a Member State has failed to fulfil a Treaty obligation).

4.9.3 EU external human rights

1. With regard to development policy the EU is the largest donor in the world, accounting for 55% of development assistance and under the 'European Consensus' policy Article 13 provides that in its dialogue with the third world it will promote common values of respect for:
- human rights;
- fundamental freedoms;
- peace;
- democracy;
- good governance;
- gender equality;
- the rule of law;
- solidarity;
- justice.

2. This 2005 development policy up-dates the previous 2000 plan in light of:
- advancement of Millennium policy goals;
- security considerations following 9/11;
- increased impact of globalisation.

3. In the case of foreign policy the EU adopts a wide range of approaches to encourage and develop human rights in its external relations, including:
   - working out common strategies and positions and co-operating in joint actions;
   - making concerted *demarches* (moves or steps in political or diplomatic affairs) and declarations;
   - ensuring that human rights clauses are inserted in international agreements;
   - project funding especially via the European Initiative for Democratisation and Human Rights (EIDHR).

4. Potential acceding states have to comply with the Copenhagen criteria which means that candidate countries must have:
   - stable institutions guaranteeing democracy;
   - observance and practice procedures of human rights and the rule of law;
   - respect for and protect minorities;
   - a functioning market economy.

5. These criteria have been developed and amplified over the years and were applied to the various waves of accession that allowed the EU to grow to its present 27 Member States.

6. Currently candidate states which commenced accession talks in 2005 are:
   - Croatia (may join 2009);
   - Turkey (may join 2013).

7. Other potential candidate states 'waiting in the wings' are:
   - Albania;
   - Bosnia;
   - Macedonia;
   - Montenegro;
   - Serbia.

8. On the opening day for signature 20 March 2007 the EU signed the UN treaty on disability rights, the first time the EU has signed a core UN human rights convention.

9. The objective of the treaty is to ensure that people with disabilities enjoy human rights and fundamental freedoms on an equal basis with everyone else.
10. The treaty provides protection for some 50 million EU citizens and an estimated 650 million people world wide.

CHAPTER 5

Themes

5.1 Indigenous peoples

1. The UN has estimated that there are some 300 million people inhabiting large areas of the globe who can be described as indigenous or aboriginal ie:
   - descendants of the original inhabitants of a country or geographical area who were there prior to external settlement or colonisation;
   - nearly always dominated by latecomers through conquest, occupation, settlement or otherwise.
2. Examples of indigenous peoples include:
   - Mayas of Guatemala and Aymaras of Bolivia;
   - Inuit and Aleutians of the circumpolar region (formerly called Eskimos);
   - Saami of Northern Europe;

- Aborigines of Australia and Maoris of New Zealand.
3. The problems of indigenous people demonstrate fundamental and universal aspects of human rights, involving among other things:
   - culture;
   - economics;
   - political rights;
   - social security;
   - fair treatment.
4. American Indians, now referred to as native Americans, first approached the League of Nations for help in the 1920s, but nothing was done until 1970 when the UN Sub-Commission on Prevention of Discrimination and Protection of Minorities recommended a study should be undertaken, the final report being made in 1984.
5. It dealt with various human rights matters including:
   - defining indigenous peoples;
   - the role of government and NGOs;
   - establishing basic rights principles;
   - specific areas of action including health, education, housing, language, culture and legal institutions.
6. In 1982 ECOSOC set up the Working Group on Indigenous Populations which has two formal tasks, to:
   - review national developments pertaining to the promotion and protection of rights and freedoms of indigenous peoples;
   - develop international standards concerning their rights, taking account of similarities and differences in their situations and aspirations throughout the world.
7. The Working Group produced a draft rights declaration, which was submitted to the Commission on Human Rights for consideration, resulting in the International Decade of the World's Indigenous People 1995–2004.
8. In May 2002 a Permanent Forum on Indigenous Issues was established with a mandate to address indigenous issues relating to:

- economic and social development;
- culture;
- the environment;
- health and education;
- human rights.

9. a) The Seventh Session took place 21 April – 2 May 2008 where the special themes were climate change, bio-cultural diversity and livelihoods, and the stewardship role of indigenous peoples and new challenges;

b) On October 24, 2007 the Human Rights Council decided to extend the mandate of the Special Rapporteur on the situation of human rights and fundamental freedoms of indigenous peoples for a period of three years.

5.2 Abolition of slavery

5.2.1 Background

1. The history of slavery is almost as old as the history of mankind and slavery still exists in the world, despite national and international abolition.

2. The English entered the slave trade in 1562 when a cargo of slaves was taken from Sierra Leone by Sir John Hawkins and sold in St Domingo.

3. Charles II awarded a charter to a company that took 3,000 slaves per year to the West Indies, and other charters followed.

4. In 1770 Britain was responsible for over half the 100,000 slaves being transported from West Africa each year, and by 1791 the trade involved more than 160 ships and 5,500 sailors.

5.2.2 Abolition

1. In 1776 the first Parliamentary motion against slavery was introduced by David Hartley, and William Wilberforce began his crusade in 1787, suffering many defeats in trying to overcome entrenched economic interests that relied on slavery.

2. He introduced annual motions in the House of Commons for abolition of the slave trade up to the year 1800, despite the unpopularity it caused him.

3. This led to the Abolition of the Slave Trade Act 1807 but it only abolished the trade, not the institution of slavery.

4. America and Denmark followed suit with other states – France, Spain and the Netherlands – being unable to trade because of the wars then taking place, although Portugal's slave trade continued.

5. A renewed Anti-Slavery Society was formed in 1823, members including Henry Brougham and William Wilberforce.

6. The Slavery Abolition Act 1833 provided that former slaves were to serve an apprenticeship to their previous masters of seven years. The taxpayer compensated former masters, with a total of £20 million sterling, the Bishop of Exeter, for example, receiving compensation of £12,700 for his 665 slaves.

5.2.3 Modern slavery and forced labour

1. Following several previous General Acts and Conventions and under League of Nations auspices the Slavery Convention entered into force 9 March 1927.

2. Article 1 provided two important definitions:
   - Slavery is the status or condition of a person over whom any or all of the powers attaching to the right of ownership are exercised.
   - The slave trade includes all acts involved in the capture, acquisition or disposal of a person with intent to reduce him to slavery … or selling or exchanging him and generally all acts of trade or transport.

3. The High Contracting Parties agreed to:
   - prevent, suppress and bring about its abolition;

- suppress trading from their territorial waters and assist each other in these endeavours.
4. Despite slavery being *jus cogens* there were provisions that:
   - allowed states to exclude some of their territories (Article 9);
   - denounce the Convention (Article 10);
5. In 1957 the Supplementary Convention on the Abolition of Slavery, the Slave Trade, and Institutions and Practices Similar to Slavery entered into force, because of further considerations:
   - progress had been made since 1926 but slavery, the slave trade and similar practices still existed;
   - the 1926 Convention remained in force but augmentation of effort was needed at national and international level;
   - there had been a Forced Labour Convention in 1930 and subsequent action by the International Labour Organisation (ILO);
   - The UN had replaced the League of Nations and the Universal Declaration promulgated.
6. Under Article 9 no reservations were allowed and it came into force promptly as only two signatories were required (Article 13).
7. 2007 marked the 200th anniversary since Britain abolished the trans-Atlantic slave trade, but slavery and forced labour are still rife in the modern world
8. It has been estimated that in 2006:
   - one in five of the world's children between 5 and 17 were involved in child labour;
   - 74 million children were involved in hazardous work that should be made to cease forthwith;
   - 8.4 million children were actually in slavery, trafficking, debt bondage and other forms of forced labour the worst kinds of which include:
     - forced recruitment for armed conflict;
     - prostitution;
     - pornography.

9. Statistics produced or quoted in 2007 by the Joseph Rowntree Foundation accept that figures are difficult to estimate, acknowledge that it is widely accepted that numbers are under-estimated, and indicate that:
   - there are at least 5,000 child sex workers in the UK, many trafficked from Eastern Europe;
   - worldwide it is estimated that there are at least 12 million people working as slaves;
   - the ILO estimates that the worldwide traffic in human beings is worth at least $32 billion annually;
   - ILO and UNICEF figures for 2004 suggest that 218 million children were trapped in labour worldwide.
10. In 2003 Romanian journalists paid $400 to buy a teenage girl, and it was claimed that girls could be purchased for $100 or $200 in Timisoara, Romania, graphically illustrating the ongoing problem of slavery.

5.3 Abolition of the death penalty

1. The death penalty has been the ultimate punishment or sanction since prehistory, used in different ways, eg:
   - as a crude form of terror;
   - imposing discipline on society through judicial execution;
   - as a means of coercing citizens eg forcing them to take up arms;
   - belief that it acts as a deterrent.
2. In humanitarian law the Geneva Conventions by common Article 3:
   a) codify customary international law;
   b) prohibit sentencing and executions without guaranteed previous judgments of a properly constituted court.
3. Global human rights documents recognise the right to life as the:
   a) UDHR 1948 proclaimed the right to life;
   b) ICCPR 1966:

- set out the principle that no one should be arbitrarily deprived of life;
- said that where the death penalty has not been abolished it should only apply to the most serious crimes;

c) 1989 Protocol to the ICCPR abolished the death penalty in peacetime.

4. Regional provisions include the:

a) European Convention 1950, under which no one was to be deprived of life intentionally apart from court sentence following conviction of (impliedly) serious crime;

- Protocol 6 (1983) Article 1 provides that the death penalty shall be abolished and that no one shall be condemned to such penalty or executed;
- States are allowed under the Protocol Article 2 to make provision in their laws for the death penalty in times of war or imminent threat of war;
- Under Articles 3 and 4 no derogations or reservations are allowed from Protocol 6

b) American Convention on Human Rights 1969, reflecting the terms of the 1966 UN Covenants, later supplemented by an additional protocol.

5. Despite widespread abolition capital punishment is still carried out by some regimes including the United States, China, Saudi Arabia and various African states.

6. Although the trend has been towards abolition over the last 60 years or so it is possible that most people do not agree, believing it either to be a deterrent or the suitable punishment for serious transgression.

7. Arguments in favour of abolition include the following:

- people are wrongly convicted and mistakes made are irrevocable;
- it is not a deterrent, even though this might seem counter intuitive;
- it allows no element of repentance, redemption or reform;

- it comprises revenge rather than punishment or protection for society.
8. The December 2006 execution of Saddam Hussein with its attendant publicity exemplifies the horror both of crime perpetrators and their own execution.

5.4 Genocide, crimes against humanity and war crimes

5.4.1 Background

1. Genocide was the term invented by the Polish jurist Raphael Lemkin during the Second World War to define a crime committed by mankind for countless generations:
   - Greek 'genos' = race or tribe;
   - Latin 'cide' = killer or act of killing.
2. The roots of the post Second World War genocide regime grew out of the First World War because:
   - genocide, although not then so named, had been committed by Turks against Armenians during that war;
   - this led to bilateral and multilateral treaties after the Great War attempting to prevent repetition;
   - unsuccessful attempts were made to try German leaders for war crimes and later to establish an International Criminal Court;
   - no substantial distinction had been made between what are now separate crimes against humanity and genocide.
3. In the Second World War more determined efforts were made to address the problem and in 1943 specific steps were taken including:
   - establishing the UN Commission for the Investigation of War Crimes;
   - issuing the Moscow Declaration referring to evidence of atrocities, massacres and mass executions.
4. After the war the Allies agreed that states must be held responsible for atrocities committed against their *own*

populations and 'atrocities' became in due course 'crimes against humanity' which included:

- murder;
- extermination;
- enslavement;
- deportation and other inhuman acts committed against civilian populations.

5. The Agreement for the Prosecution and Punishment of Major War Criminals of the European Axis and Establishing the Charter of the International Military Tribunal was adopted by the four major allies, the US, UK, France and Russia in August 1945, and 19 other states accepted the treaty while playing no part in the trials.

6. In the Nuremberg trial of the major war criminals:

- 24 were indicted;
- 19 were convicted;
- death sentences were imposed in 12 cases.

5.4.2 The modern position

1. Groups protected by the UN Convention on the Prevention and Punishment of the Crime of Genocide are:

- national;
- racial;
- ethnical;
- religious.

2. Groups excluded from protection include:

- political;
- ideological;
- linguistic;
- economic.

3. This is problematic, as many horrific events fall outside the definition resulting in attempts being made to:

a) include within the definition events that are not, thus risking discrediting the Convention;

b) extend the boundaries of the definition.

4. These crimes invoke the notion of 'group rights' contrasting with a usual core feature of Western rights that they are primarily individual and personal.

5. Genocide can be committed in many ways, eg:
   - killing;
   - causing serious bodily or mental harm;
   - inflicting conditions of life calculated to bring about physical destruction;
   - imposing measures intended to prevent births;
   - forcibly removing or transferring children.

6. Crimes against humanity can be committed by:
   - murder;
   - deportation or forcible transfer of population;
   - imprisonment or other severe deprivation of physical liberty;
   - torture;
   - rape, forced prostitution, pregnancy or sterilisation;
   - enforced disappearance of persons;
   - apartheid;

7. War crimes arise in varying contexts eg:
   - torture;
   - inhuman treatment or biological experiments;
   - destruction and expropriation of property;
   - denying a fair trial;
   - unlawful deportation and transfer;
   - hostage taking, attacking civilians or civilian objects.

8. Some actions may be both crimes against humanity and war crimes.

9. Tackling these group crimes is riddled with inconsistency and wholesale violations are tolerated because of reluctance to become involved unless some vital state interests are prejudiced.

5.5 Humanitarian intervention and peace keeping

1. Humanitarian intervention can be defined as armed intervention by one or more states in another state's affairs:
   - without that state's agreement;
   - with the intention of preventing actual or threatened humanitarian disaster; especially when caused by widespread human rights violations.
2. The four essential elements are:
   a) genuine humanitarian intention;
   b) actual and severe breaches of human rights;
   c) breach of sovereignty of the state being invaded;
   d) armed intervention.
3. Article 24(1) and Chapter VII of the UN Charter give the SC power to take measures necessary to restore international peace and security and with this authority humanitarian intervention is possible and legal.
4. By Article 24(1), members:
   - confer on the SC primary responsibility for maintenance of international peace and security;
   - agree that in carrying out its duty under this responsibility the SC acts on their behalf;
   - concede that the justification provided by the article is to ensure prompt and effective action by the UN.
5. Chapter VII comprises Articles 39–51 inclusive of the Charter and covers:
   - actions threatening peace;
   - actual breaches of the peace;
   - acts of aggression.
6. Whenever such action is contemplated, in addition to Article 24(1) and Chapter VII, Article 2 of the Charter also needs to be considered as it:
   - proclaims principles of sovereign equality;
   - requires good faith in carrying out obligations;
   - insists on settlement of international disputes by

peaceful means without risking peace, security and justice;

- disallows threat or use of force against territorial integrity or political independence of other states;
- says that nothing contained in the Charter authorises the UN to intervene in matters that are essentially within the domestic jurisdiction of any state.

7. The state sovereignty doctrine is important as it provides the main restraint on stronger states taking advantage of weaker ones, so all breaches of sovereignty are potentially dangerous to stability.

8. Problems thus arise as to the best approach to take given the wide variety of circumstances that may arise, the main choices being to leave well alone or interfere to protect people or redress perceived wrongs, which process requires a balance between sovereignty and human rights.

9. A distinction should be drawn between humanitarian intervention and peace keeping operations, the latter usually referring to a UN presence involving a number of characteristics including:

- use of a combination of civilian and military personnel;
- consent of conflicting parties;
- attempts to bring about conflict resolution;
- assisting delivery of humanitarian aid to the civilian population.

10. The UN have categorised peace keeping in three ways:

- assistance in maintenance of ceasefires, eg separating fighting forces to facilitate diplomatic processes to proceed;
- implementation of comprehensive settlements, eg encouraging integration back to normal life and assisting with free elections;
- as a means of providing protection for humanitarian operations, the purpose here being to alleviate human suffering.

11. There is no recognised regime extant clearly stating what the ground rules should be for humanitarian intervention

but possible criteria include:
- threat or occurrence of serious and extensive human rights violations;
- adequate proven evidence of this with an urgent need to act;
- refusal to remedy or prevent the violations;
- limiting the action to removing the threat or preventing abuse;
- extensive support for the action from victims and neighbours;
- force only used as a last resort with no breaches of the laws of war and a good chance of success;
- clear and unambiguous UN authority and a post-conflict restoration plan.

12. These considerations are vital to:
- maximise support and legitimacy;
- minimise damage and adverse consequences;
- uphold human rights.

13. In the 1990s there were a number of interventions involving some humanitarian rationalisation eg:
- Kosovo;
- East Timor;
- Sierra Leone.

14. Since the end of the Cold War the question has arisen of whether a group of states with authority falling short of the above criteria is justified in undertaking humanitarian intervention, and whether it can be used as a fall-back reason when previously stated justifications fail, eg actions taken by NATO.

15. Steps short of intervention can be used including:
- criticism by governments, NGOs and INGOs;
- diplomatic pressure;
- economic sanctions;
- supplying aid and humanitarian assistance.

5.6 Apartheid

5.6.1 South Africa

1. This Afrikaans word was first used by Jan Smuts in 1917 two years before he became Prime Minister of South Africa:
   - its literal translation is 'aparthood';
   - translated into English this means apartness or separation.

2. Today it means a legally sanctioned system of ethnic segregation such as existed in South Africa between 1948 and 1990.

3. It is antithetic to primary norms of human rights universality and negates or denies provisions of instruments such as the International Bill of Human Rights.

4. Apologists for apartheid claim that it prevents minority races from being swamped by numerically superior races and if properly applied allows fair treatment of all sectors of society.

5. In practice it contravenes legal and human rights norms because it:
   a) produces a hierarchy of races;
   b) enforces by law widespread segregation on society eg for:
      - work;
      - marriage;
      - residence.
   c) arrogates to the ruling class and race the bulk of the state's resources and assets.

6. South Africa suffered many adverse effects eg:
   - non-whites were excluded from national government and full voting rights;
   - they were not allowed to operate businesses in white-only areas;
   - they comprised 70 per cent of the population but were confined to small segregated parts of the country and forced to carry passes;

- workers and their families were separated, with public transport and other facilities being segregated;
- their land was inferior and their townships squalid;
- in virtually all aspects of their lives, blacks were kept away from and under inferior conditions to whites.

7. Apartheid was introduced in South Africa after the National Party won the 1948 general election. The racial legislation included:
   - Prohibition of Mixed Marriages Act 1949;
   - Reservation of Separate Amenities Act 1953;
   - Bantu Education Act 1953;
   - Black Homeland Citizenship Act 1971.

8. Increasing protests throughout the 1950s eventually led to the Sharpville demonstration against the Pass Law (requirement to carry identity cards) in March 1960 where police killed 69 demonstrators and injured 180.

9. UN General Assembly Resolution 1761 was passed on 6 November 1962 condemning apartheid and calling on other states to terminate military and economic relations with South Africa.

10. Nelson Mandela was sentenced to life imprisonment in 1964 and South Africa gradually became more isolated while repeated resolutions passed at the UN condemned racism, including World Conferences Against Racism in 1978 and 1983.

11. In 1984 some reforms were instituted and when F W de Klerk succeeded P W Botha as president in 1989 the end was in sight, the ban on the ANC being lifted in 1990, Mandela being released from prison, and repeal of the remaining apartheid laws.

12. In 2003 President Thabo Mbeki announced that 660 million rand (US$85 million) would be used to recompense approximately 22,000 people who had been tortured, imprisoned or who had lost relatives during the apartheid era.

5.6.2 The UN Convention on Apartheid

1. The International Convention on the Suppression and Punishment of the Crime of Apartheid:
   - was adopted and opened for signature and ratification by General Assembly resolution 3068 (XXVIII) of 30 November 1973;
   - comprised 19 articles and entered into force in accordance with Article XV on 18 July 1976.
2. Article I declares apartheid to be a crime against humanity as well as violating principles of international law and the UN Charter, and under Article II the commission of inhuman acts that come within the definition of the crime include:
   a) denial to a member or members of racial groups the right to life and liberty of person by:
      - murder;
      - infliction of serious bodily or mental harm;
      - arbitrary arrest and illegal imprisonment.
   b) deliberate imposition on a racial group of living conditions calculated to cause apartheid or their physical destruction in whole or in part;
   c) legislative and other measures calculated to prevent racial groups from participating in the political, social, economic and cultural life of the country;
   d) any measures designed to divide the population along racial lines:
      - by creating reserves or ghettos;
      - prohibiting mixed marriages;
      - expropriating property belonging to racial groups.
3. Other articles address:
   - international criminal responsibility;
   - amendment of state laws;
   - trial by competent tribunals;
   - submission of periodic reports and supervision by the Commission on Human Rights;
   - exclusion of these crimes from political designation so as to avoid extradition.

5.7 Truth commissions

1. Commissions of Inquiry are used for many purposes; out of these have grown truth commissions in at least 25 states from Argentina to Zimbabwe, and although they differ markedly from one place and purpose to another they tend to have a number of features in common which include:
   - researching and reporting on human rights abuses over particular turbulent periods in states where the rule of law has broken down;
   - taking evidence from survivors, relatives and perpetrators about what happened in a forum which is outside the usual state judicial apparatus;
   - reaching conclusions as to fact and making a final report containing recommendations to prevent future recurrence of abuses;
   - bearing the authority of the state's current regime, sometimes established with the assistance of international organisations.

2. They vary considerably with regard to:
   - precise mandate terms;
   - processes and procedures adopted;
   - use made of conclusions;
   - effectiveness

3. An early modern example was the commission set up in Argentina following the Falklands War, not directly because of the war, but because defeat led to the removal of military government and desire to identify previous misuse of power.

4. The National Commission on the Disappeared:
   - was established by President Raul Alfonsin in 1983 and comprised ten members;
   - published its report in September 1984 on 9,000 disappearances occurring during military rule from 1976–83.

5. Perhaps the best known truth commission is the South African Commission established in 1995 by the South

African parliament to investigate human rights abuses during apartheid between 1960 to 1994:

- its chairman was Archbishop Desmond Tutu and it had 17 members, holding public meetings throughout South Africa;
- the amnesty committee processed over 7,000 applications by perpetrators who in return for confessions were granted immunity from prosecution;
- the reparation and rehabilitation committee recommended appropriate compensation with the final report being presented to President Nelson Mandela in October 1998.

6. After the reunification of Germany, a 27-member Study Commission for the Assessment of History and Consequences of the SED Dictatorship in Germany:
   - was established by the German parliament in 1992;
   - investigated human rights violations under communist rule between 1949 and 1989.

7. One of the principal reasons for having truth commissions rather than criminal trials is to achieve 'closure' for survivors and relatives by finding out the truth, rather than convicting a few perpetrators.

8. Other relatively successful truth commissions were those for Chile and El Salvador, but not all are satisfactory, eg:
   - The Guatemalan conflict was brought to an end but the commission's terms were extremely narrow;
   - Uganda failed to complete theirs because of lack of funding and political will.

9. Truth Commissions may operate strictly within states' own frameworks, but they nearly all draw heavily on global human rights norms and are characterised by:
   - real desire for change;
   - need to resolve issues and put the past behind them;
   - desire to address issues of amnesty, forgiveness and compensation.

CHAPTER 6

European Human
Rights

6.1 The beginnings

6.1.1 Post-Second World War Europe

1. European regional human rights began after the Second World War.
2. Germany was divided into zones between the four main allies: the US, USSR, France and the UK.

3. Eastern Europe was dominated by the Soviets and kept under tight control, Hungary (1956) and Czechoslovakia (1968) being invaded when they stepped out of line.
4. Western Europe was relatively free but opposing ideologies led to nearly 50 years of 'Cold War'.
5. The two power blocs reorganised themselves into defensive alliances in light of the new circumstances, the West forming NATO and the East the Warsaw Pact.
6. The war left huge reconstruction problems:
   • American aid of $4.34 billion (modern equivalent £27 billion) was given to the UK under the Marshall Plan in 1947;
   • final repayment was made in 2006 of £43 million to the US and £12 million to Canada.
7. The Organisation for European Cooperation was established in 1948.

6.1.2 The legacy of war crimes

1. Nazi atrocities during the war resulted in war crimes tribunals at Nuremberg and Tokyo, the former established by the Charter of the International Military Tribunal in August 1945.
2. The Allies tried and punished by death or imprisonment a number of individuals under three main categories:
   a) crimes against peace;
   b) war crimes;
   c) crimes against humanity.
3. One problem was that when murderous acts were perpetrated during the war it was not thought that states could commit crimes against their own citizens.
4. The principles of international law established by the Military Charter and judgment were adopted in 1950 by the International Law Commission of the United Nations.
5. The Tokyo trials were heavily criticised as being more akin to victor's justice than were the Nuremberg trials.

6. Some of the atrocities committed were so egregious that new descriptions or categories were invented, including Lemkin's 'genocide' in 1943.

6.1.3 The European response

1. One reason for the failure of the League of Nations was lack of support by influential nations but another significant factor was that human rights were ignored by the League.
2. The Allies determined that the new global regime, the United Nations, would avoid this mistake, so human rights comprised a vital ingredient in the organisation and its organs.
3. As both world conflicts had originated in Europe, many European states believed that in addition to the UN there had to be a specific European response concentrating on human rights.
4. During 1948–9 international negotiations led to the founding of a new organisation to encourage peace and good relations over and above short-term self-interested political, economic and military objectives, to be achieved by a Committee of participating government ministers with a consultative assembly, which eventually became the Council of Europe whose statute was signed in London on 5 May 1949.

6.1.4 The British response

1. The British government supported the Council and idea of a Convention to encourage human rights in Europe but did not think it was necessary for the UK to become too closely involved because:
   • it was considered that the common law was superior to continental civil law;
   • common law remedies such as habeas corpus and jury trial were felt to be adequate to protect citizens;

- they failed to understand the end of the empire and the need for closer ties with Europe.

2. Britain therefore initially decided against allowing its citizens to bring complaints before the newly established Commission on Human Rights.

6.2 The Council of Europe

Council of Europe 1948

Committee of Ministers

European Commission of Human Rights 1954

European Court of Human Rights 1959

Reconstituted European Court 1998
Type 'HUDOC' into your search engine for a detailed database

6.2.1 Council of Europe institutions

1. The Congress of Europe met in The Hague in 1948 to establish the Council of Europe with objectives that included:

- upholding the rule of law;
- fostering human rights;
- drafting a charter of human rights.

2. The three main institutions of the Council of Europe were the:
   - European Commission on Human Rights established in 1954;
   - European Court of Human Rights established in 1959 and reconstituted in 1998, sitting in Strasbourg;
   - Committee of Ministers of the Council of Europe whose members are the foreign ministers of the 47 Member States.

3. The Council of Europe is distinct from the European Union (EU), formerly known as the Common Market and then the European Economic Community (EEC).

4. Nevertheless, joining the Council of Europe and acceding to the European Convention of Human Rights are pre-requisites to EU membership because of the minimum standards of human rights conduct they set.

6.2.2 Development of European Human Rights

1. The Committee of Ministers meets six times a year to ensure that the Court's judgments are carried out (Article 46 amended by Protocol 11).

2. The ministers' or their deputies' other duties include reviewing various aspects of human rights such as:
   - anti-racism;
   - abolition of the death penalty;
   - reformation or up-dating of the Convention.

3. Prior to 1998 the *Commission* decided on admissibility of human rights applications but because the system was slow, overloaded and generally unsatisfactory, the *Court* was reconstituted and became full-time in November 1998, now dealing with admissibility and substantive hearings (Protocol 11).

4. The Court has the same number of judges as there are Member States (currently 47) but there is no rule that every state must be represented by a judge.

6.3 European Convention principles

6.3.1 Characteristics of the Convention

Basic facts about the Convention are:
1. It has international treaty status and its full title is the Convention for the Protection of Human Rights and Fundamental Freedoms.
2. Signed in November 1950, it entered into force September 3, 1953.
3. The emphasis is on individual and political rights rather than collective economic, social and cultural rights.
4. These tend to represent western ideas of personal freedom as opposed to:
   - Soviet bloc economic and social objectives (in Cold War terms); or
   - Third World aspirations of developmental, educational or health rights.

6.3.2 UK involvement

1. The UK was one of the founding members and played a crucial role in drafting the treaty, but declined to incorporate it into UK law in 1953.
2. The Labour Party made an electoral commitment in 1997 to introduce the Convention into domestic law and to 'bring rights home'.
3. The Human Rights Act was passed in 1998 and came into effect in October 2000 to allow direct enforcement without having to take cases to Strasbourg, although this still remains an option once domestic routes are exhausted.

6.4 Types of Convention rights

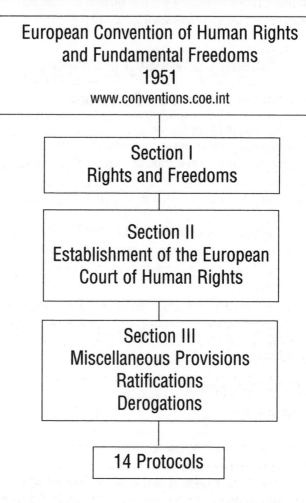

European Convention of Human Rights
and Fundamental Freedoms
1951
www.conventions.coe.int

Section I
Rights and Freedoms

Section II
Establishment of the European
Court of Human Rights

Section III
Miscellaneous Provisions
Ratifications
Derogations

14 Protocols

6.4.1 Categories of rights and reservations

There are a number of categories of Convention rights:
1. Non-derogable rights ie Articles 2, 3, 4(1) and 7.
2. Other rights, ie Articles 4(2), 5, 6, 9(1) and 12, together
   with Protocol 1, Articles 2 and 3, and Protocol 6 Article 1.

3. Qualified rights comprising the remainder, ie Articles 8, 9, 10 and 11.
4. Derogations and reservations.

6.4.2 Non-derogable rights

1. These are the most strongly protected rights, not to be restricted even in times of emergency or war.
2. There are special provisions dealing with the death penalty and capital punishment as unanimity could not be reached on those matters.
3. Apart from these public interest cannot be used to curtail or interfere with basic rights, even including action against terrorism or organised crime (*Selmouni v France* (1999)).
4. The four non-derogable rights are:
   • prohibition against torture;
   • prohibition against slavery and forced labour;
   • no punishment without law;
   • right to life.
5. Only the prohibition against torture or inhuman or degrading treatment is absolutely unqualified (ie can be described as 'absolute') but even these are open to interpretation.
6. Right to life is qualified by Convention provisions acknowledging exceptions of:
   • self-defence;
   • arrest;
   • prevention of escape from lawful custody;
   • quelling riots or insurrection.
7. Prohibition of slavery and forced labour is qualified by Convention provisions recognising work required during:
   • lawful imprisonment;
   • military service (or conscientious objection alternatives);
   • work required to counter emergencies;
   • disaster work recognised as comprising part of normal civic obligations.

8. The requirement of 'no punishment without law' is qualified in that:
   - it must not prejudice trial and punishment of people for acts or omissions which, when committed, were criminal according to general principles of law recognised by civilised nations;
   - it guards against retrospective criminal laws and prevents heavier sentences being imposed than applied when the offence was committed (*Welch v UK* (1995));
   - if changes are foreseeable as in progressive attitudes to marital rape, the qualification will not apply (*SW v UK* (1995)).

6.4.3 Other rights

1. There are rights which are not so strongly protected which can be restricted in emergency and war situations:
   - prohibitions on forced labour (as opposed to slavery);
   - rights to liberty and security;
   - fair trial;
   - freedom of thought, conscience and religion;
   - marriage;
   - education;
   - free elections;
   - abolition of death penalty.
2. These rights are distinguished from non-derogable ones because there is justification within the Convention text for them to be restricted in the public interest, but only to the extent provided by the Convention.

6.4.4 Qualified rights

1. For qualified rights the emphasis is more on the fact that private and public interest has to be balanced and this varies between states, so the kinds of right included are:
   - respect for private and family life;
   - manifesting religion or belief (as opposed to holding such views);

- freedom of expression, assembly and association;
- protection of property.
2. In order to qualify these rights any restriction(s) imposed must be:
   - prescribed by law;
   - legitimate;
   - necessary and proportionate;
   - not discriminatory.

6.4.5 Derogations and reservations

1. Derogation occurs under Article 15 of the Convention when a state withdraws from specified obligations because of war or other public emergency, but only so far as allowed by the exigencies involved.
2. It is not allowed in respect of:
   - right to life;
   - freedom from torture;
   - slavery and servitude;
   - retrospective criminal penalties.
3. It has been used by the UK for the Anti-Terrorism, Crime and Security Act 2001 and for detention of alleged terrorists in Northern Ireland when:
   - the European Court found against Britain in *Brogan v UK* (1988)) so the government enacted the Prevention of Terrorism (Temporary Provisions) Act 1989;
   - the derogation itself was challenged and that challenge failed (*Brannigan v UK* (1993)).
4. High Contracting Parties can enter reservations (as opposed to derogations) to particular aspects of international treaties the UK having done so in respect of educational rights contained in Protocol 1 Article 2.
5. The reservation was that the government would only observe the principle so far as was compatible with provision of efficient instructions and training and avoidance of unreasonable public expenditure.

6. Under section 16 of the Human Rights Act designated derogations cease to have effect after five years in UK domestic law unless they are renewed, but this does not apply to reservations.

6.5 Operating principles of the European Court

6.5.1 Purposive approach and proportionality

1. The European Court cannot operate legislatively or overrule the treaty, but takes a purposive or teleological approach (ie attempting to achieve the desired objective) to interpretation which may be seen as:
   - broader than the literal rule of English law statutory interpretation;
   - development of the mischief and golden rules.
2. The advantage is that it has been able to react to changing conditions in Europe over the last 50 years.
3. Because of the Convention's wide scope and diversity of national cultures the Court utilises the principle of 'proportionality' in reaching decisions, maintaining a balance between individuals' rights and legitimate state interests.
4. So it has been held that:
   - customs officers were not justified in seizing and refusing to return motor vehicles where the owners had evaded payment of duty on alcohol and tobacco (*Lindsay v Commissioners of Customs and Excise* (2002));
   - such action was disproportionate and failed to distinguish between commercial/professional smugglers and people bringing goods into the UK for personal or family use.
5. Proportionality arises because some individual rights are qualified rather than absolute, eg:
   - Article 8(1) states that 'everyone has the right to respect for his private and family life, his home and his correspondence', but,

- Article 8(2) stipulates that there should be no interference by a public authority with the exercise of this right except in accordance with law and necessary in a democratic society in the interests of the:
  - economic wellbeing of the country;
  - prevention of disorder or crime;
  - protection of health or morals;
  - protection of rights and freedoms of others;
  - national security;
  - public safety.
6. So in *Handyside v UK* (1976) it was said that every 'formality', 'condition', 'restriction' or 'penalty' imposed, where qualified rights were said to be 'necessary in a democratic society', had to be 'proportionate to the legitimate aim pursued' (paragraph 49).

6.5.2 Margin of appreciation

1. The 'margin of appreciation' doctrine allows states discretion in the extent to which they implement Convention measures:
   - the basis of the doctrine is acceptance that national bodies, governmental or judicial, are better placed than an international court to determine local needs;
   - the Court does not always insist on strict or narrow interpretation of individual rights although this doctrine does not apply in domestic law (*R v DPP ex parte Kebilene* (1999));
   - it is analogous to the EU principle of subsidiarity.
2. It will not always apply however: *Goodwin v UK* (2002) involved violations of transsexuals' rights under Articles 8 (privacy) and 12 (marriage) and the Court held that current international attitudes towards acceptance of transsexuals meant that states had to adapt their behaviour which the UK had failed to do.
3. The Convention has been interpreted to impose positive as well as negative responsibilities on states so rights of

peaceful assembly are not merely preventative duties on states but may amount to positive enabling duties (*Plattform 'Artze fur Leben' v Austria* (1988)).

6.6 Other European Conventions

1. Other separate European Conventions deal with human rights and the most important are detailed below.
2. The European Convention for the Prevention of Torture and Inhuman or Degrading Treatment or Punishment 1987 has 23 articles and two Protocols added in 1993:
   - it establishes a European Committee empowered to visit and examine the treatment of imprisoned persons with a view to protecting them from inhuman or degrading treatment or punishment;
   - it thus extends the provisions in the Convention on Human Rights and requires co-operation from competent national authorities;
   - the Protocols deal with administrative matters, and this Convention's machinery strengthens Article 3 of the ECHR.
3. The European Charter for Regional or Minority Languages 1992 and the Framework Convention for the Protection of National Minorities 1995 complement each other and are important because of Europe's ethnic diversity:
   - the former has 23 articles, Article 3 requiring states to identify and specify regional or minority languages;
   - the objectives and principles in Article 7 provide practical means to make the Convention effective, eg facilitating minority speech in public life;
   - Part III provides measures addressing educational, judicial, administrative and public authorities, media and cultural activities, together with economic and social life.
4. The 1995 National Minorities Framework promotes conditions necessary for national minorities to maintain

and develop their own cultures, including religion, language, traditions and cultural heritage (Article 5).

5. The European Convention on the Exercise of Children's Rights 1996 applies to children under 18 years of age, granting procedural rights to ensure their best interests are observed before judicial authorities:
   - the judicial authority's role is specified, with duties to act speedily to protect children;
   - a Standing Committee is established in Chapter III to keep relevant questions about the Convention under review.

6. The Convention for the Protection of Human Rights and Dignity of the Human Being with regard to the Application of Biology and Medicine, usually known as the Convention on Human Rights and Biomedicine 1997, breaks new ground including human genome, scientific research and organ and tissue removal from living donors for transplanting purposes:
   - Article 28 recognises that there are controversial and rapidly advancing issues within the Convention's ambit so that public discussion is essential;
   - the 1998 Protocol prevents human cloning with no derogation, and the 2002 Protocol protects people's dignity and identity with regard to transplantation of organs and tissues of human origin.

CHAPTER 7

The Operation of the Convention

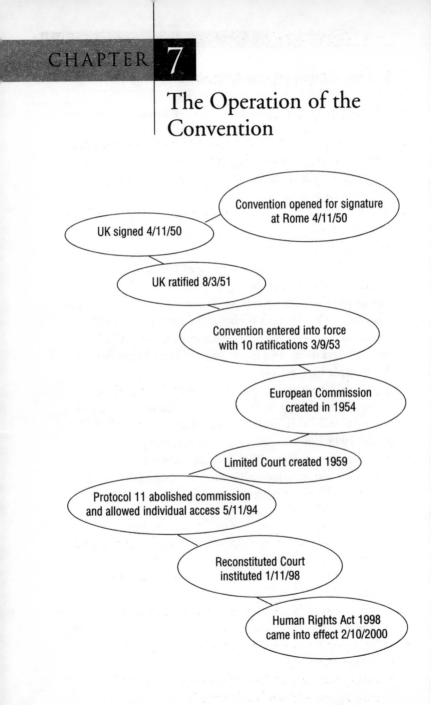

Convention opened for signature at Rome 4/11/50

UK signed 4/11/50

UK ratified 8/3/51

Convention entered into force with 10 ratifications 3/9/53

European Commission created in 1954

Limited Court created 1959

Protocol 11 abolished commission and allowed individual access 5/11/94

Reconstituted Court instituted 1/11/98

Human Rights Act 1998 came into effect 2/10/2000

THE OPERATION OF THE CONVENTION

7.1 The Convention Articles

7.1.1 Rights protected

1. The Convention for the Protection of Human Rights and Fundamental Freedoms 1950 (the European Convention on Human Rights) covers a wide range of measures, summarised below.
2. Section 1 contains the rights and freedoms in Articles 2–18 and specifically:
   a) Articles 15–18 cover:
      • derogation in times of emergency;
      • restrictions on political activity of aliens;
      • prohibition of abuse of rights;
      • limitation on the ability to restrict rights;
   b) Article 13 gives the right to an effective remedy but it was not incorporated by the Human Rights Act 1998 because:
      • it was thought the Act itself provides all the protection needed;
      • government was wary of giving excessive power to the judiciary.
3. The Convention identifies rights to:
   • life (Article 2);
   • liberty and security (Article 5);
   • fair hearings (Article 6);
   • respect for private and family life (Article 8);
   • freedom of thought, conscience and religion (Article 9);
   • expression (Article 10);
   • freedom of assembly and association (Article 11);
   • marry (Article 12);
   • effective remedy (Article 13) although this is not incorporated in UK domestic law.
4. Other rights are expressed as prohibitions against:
   • torture (Article 2);
   • slavery and forced labour (Article 3);
   • punishment without law (Article 7);

- discrimination on any ground such as sex, race, colour, language, religion, political or other opinion, national or social origin, association with a national minority, property, birth or other status (Article 14).

7.1.2 Right to life (Article 2)

1. Everyone's right to life is protected by law subject to qualifications of:
   - judicial execution;
   - self-defence;
   - effecting lawful arrest or preventing unlawful escape;
   - lawful action to quell riot or insurrection.
2. The case of *A (Children) Conjoined Twins: Surgical Separation* (2001) held that an operation to separate twins which would result in certain death of one would not be unlawful as she would die anyway and it was the only way the other could survive.
3. There is no correlative right to die (*R (Pretty) v DPP* (2002)) and subsequently in the European Court, where a mentally competent but physically incapable woman was refused an assurance that her husband could legally help her to die.
4. In an earlier case the Commission declared inadmissible a husband's application to prevent his wife from obtaining an abortion, the life of the unborn foetus being considered more closely connected to the mother (also see *C v S* (1987)).
5. States have a positive obligation to take appropriate steps to:
   - safeguard the lives of those within their jurisdiction (*Mahmut Kaya v Turkey* (2000));
   - take reasonable steps to prevent suicide while in custody (*Keenan v UK* (1998)).

7.1.3 Prohibition of torture (Article 3)

1. There is an unqualified prohibition against subjection to torture or to inhuman or degrading treatment or punishment.

2. Torture is defined in *Ireland v UK* (1978) as deliberate inhuman treatment causing very serious and cruel suffering:
   - inhuman treatment is less severe but may include threats of torture, psychological harm, and physical assault;
   - the perpetrator's behavioural threshold is lowered if the complainant is in custody;
   - degrading treatment is punishment arousing in the victim feelings of fear, anguish and inferiority capable of debasing the victim or breaking his or her moral resistance;
   - vulnerability of the victim is a relevant factor.

3. The European Court held in *Ireland v UK* that Northern Ireland security forces' techniques did not amount to torture but did constitute inhuman treatment that was also degrading by:
   - forcing victims to stand against walls for long periods;
   - hooding suspects;
   - subjecting them to noise;
   - depriving them of sleep, food and drink.

4. In *Tyrer v UK* (1980), birching a 15-year-old boy in humiliating circumstances breached Article 3.

5. Imposing additional punishment on a prisoner and insufficient monitoring of his known mental condition leading to his suicide was inhuman and degrading treatment and breached Article 3 (*Keenan v UK* (2001)).

7.1.4 Prohibition of slavery (Article 4)

1. Article 4 says that no one shall be held in slavery or servitude or be required to perform forced or compulsory labour with the following exemptions:
   - work done while in detention;
   - military service;
   - work exacted in times of emergency or calamity threatening life or wellbeing of the community;
   - work or service forming part of normal civic obligations.

2. Neither slavery nor servitude are defined by the European Convention but the 1926 Slavery Convention defines slavery in Article 1(1) as the status or condition of a person over whom any or all of the powers attaching to the right of ownership are exercised.

3. Servitude was explained in *Van Droogenbroek v Belgium* (1982) as the obligation to provide another with services (and) the obligation on the part of the 'serf' to live on another's property with the impossibility of changing his condition.

4. In that case a 30-year-old convicted thief was sentenced (in addition to two years' imprisonment) to being placed at the Government's disposal for 10 years, but his claim was rejected by the European Court.

7.1.5 Right to liberty and security (Article 5)

1. This right is limited, the operative words being that everyone has the right to liberty and security of person (and) no one shall be deprived of his liberty.

2. However, specified exceptions include:
   - lawful arrest and imprisonment in a variety of circumstances;
   - detention to avoid spread of disease;
   - arrest of persons of unsound mind, alcoholics, drug addicts and vagrants.

3. The circumstances listed in Article 5 are exhaustive and cannot be added to (*Ireland v UK* (1980)).

4. Ideas of political correctness change over time so detention of vagrants may nowadays be inappropriate.

5. Distinguishing between deprivation of liberty and restrictions on freedom is difficult involving degree or intensity rather than nature or substance (*Guzzardi v Italy* (1980)).

6. In *Steel v UK* (1999) the European Court considered several English cases where there had been detention and conviction for breaches of the peace in a variety of

circumstances and held that these were offences within Article 5(1)(c), so the arrests were lawful and not in contravention of Article 5.

7. By way of contrast the applicants in *Hashman and Harrup v UK* (2000) ruined a fox hunt by blowing a misleading horn to distract the hounds and the:
   - Crown Court said that they had behaved in a manner *contra bonos mores* (against good standards of behaviour) and bound them over to keep the peace even though there had been no actual breach of the peace;
   - European Court said that such vagueness was not a procedure prescribed by law as no one could predict what standards of good behaviour a future court might expect.

7.1.6 Right to a fair trial (Article 6)

1. The description 'fair *trial*' is a misnomer because the article refers to the determination of civil rights and the obligations of a criminal charge within a reasonable time and by an independent and impartial tribunal established by law, so 'fair *hearing*' might be preferable.

2. The article establishes other essential criteria for fairness such as public pronouncement of verdicts and decisions, and presumption of innocence, although secrecy is allowable where the following justifications apply:
   - morality;
   - public order;
   - national security;
   - protection of juveniles;
   - protection of parties' private lives.

3. Minimum rights are specified for everyone charged with a criminal offence including the:
   - right to be informed of the nature of the accusation promptly in a language that he can understand;
   - provision of adequate time and facilities to prepare a defence;
   - ability to defend oneself either in person or with legal assistance;

- examination of witnesses and use of interpretation services if needed.

4. Legitimate reasons for excluding the public from hearings include:
   - sexual offences against children (*X v Austria* (1965));
   - divorce (*X v UK* (1977));
   - medical patients' privacy (*Guenoun v France* (1990)).

5. So the basic rule is that:
   - courts should sit in public session unless and until a legitimate reason for privacy arises (*Diennet v France* (1995));
   - exceptions must be justifiable and proportionate (*Schuler-Zgraggen v Switzerland* (1993)).

6. To ensure fairness parties should usually be present in court when civil rights and obligations are to be determined, particularly when factual or personal issues have to be resolved eg *X v Sweden* (1959).

7. 'Equality of arms' means maintaining a balance between the prosecutor and accused, eg providing legal aid or translation services to ensure that a defendant is not unfairly prejudiced by the power and resources of the prosecution.

8. The same principle applies to civil proceedings although the requirements of fairness are less strict as parties are more likely to be equally balanced (*Dombo Beheer v Netherlands* (1993)).

9. Other important elements of fair hearings are that:
   - there should be no undue delay, everyone under Article 6(1) being entitled to a fair and public hearing within a reasonable time;
   - in assessing reasonableness the court considers the:
     - conduct of the applicant and relevant authorities;
     - complexity of the case;
     - importance of the matter to the applicant.

10. Avoiding delay is important for:
    - children (*H v UK* (1987));
    - employment disputes (*Nibbio v Italy* (1992));

- cases involving serious personal injuries or old age
(*Dewicka v Poland* (2000)).

7.1.7 No punishment without law (Article 7)

1. This article aims to prevent the creation of retrospective
offences and increased penalties and is connected to
Protocol 7 dealing with double jeopardy, although the UK
has not ratified this.
2. The avoidance of retrospectivity applies both to legislation
and the common law (*SW and CR v UK* (1995)).
3. Article 7(2) qualifies the rules by saying that the trial and
punishment of any person for acts or omissions which,
when committed, were criminal according to general
principles of law recognised by civilised nations, enables
novel criminal misbehaviour to be punished, the principle
deriving from Nazi war crimes made choate after the war.

7.1.8 Right to respect for private and family life (Article 8)

1. Article 8 declares that everyone has rights to respect for
private and family life, home and correspondence, without
interference by public authority, except such as is in
accordance with law and necessary in a democratic society
in the interests of the:
   - economic wellbeing of the country;
   - prevention of disorder or crime;
   - protection of health or morals;
   - protection of rights and freedoms of others;
   - national security;
   - public safety.
2. It is thus considerably qualified and connected to marriage
rights under Article 12.
3. Family life is not restricted to marriages, so unmarried
couples connected by children may qualify (*Kroon v
Netherlands* (1994)) and other factors for consideration
are:

- whether the parties live together;
- how long their relationship lasted;
- the extent to which they have demonstrated mutual commitment (*X and Y & Z v UK* (1983)).
4. Children play an important part in family life so:
   - previous ties remain even if the parents have separated (*Keegan v Ireland* (1994));
   - potential ties must be considered eg between father and illegitimate child (*Soderback v Sweden* (1998)).
5. Distinctions are drawn between family and private life so stable relationships between gay or lesbian couples may be recognised as comprising private if not family life in differing contexts eg where there is a:
   - partner threatened by deportation (*X and Y v UK* (1983));
   - claim to inherit a tenancy (*S v UK* (1986)).
6. Besides partners and children family life can extend to:
   - siblings (*Moustaquim v Belgium* (1991));
   - uncles (*Boyle v UK* (1994));
   - grandparents (*Bronda v Italy* (1998));
   - questions of access and custody (*Hendriks v Netherlands* (1983));
   - maintenance payments (*Logan v UK* (1996));
   - care proceedings (*L v Finland* (2000)).

7.1.9 Right to marry (Article 12)

1. Article 12 is related to Article 8 and says that men and women of marriageable age have the right to marry and found a family according to the national laws governing the exercise of this right.
2. Marrying is the means of establishing a legal relationship:
   - it does not require cohabitation or procreation;
   - public authorities are not entitled to prevent persons kept in custody, even under life sentence, from marrying (*Hamer v UK* (1979));
   - prisoners are not currently afforded the right to found a family.

3. The right to marry does not mean that there is a right to divorce (*Johnston and others v Ireland* (1986)) although:
   - parties are free to separate and not be obliged to live together (*Airey v Ireland* (1979));
   - there should be no unreasonable restrictions on divorcees preventing them from remarrying (*F v Switzerland* (1987)).
4. The right to marry is also recognised under Article 23 of the International Covenant on Civil and Political Rights.

7.1.10 Freedom of thought, conscience and religion (Article 9)

1. Rights to freedom of thought, conscience and religion includes freedom to:
   - change religion;
   - manifest it in worship, teaching, practice and observance.
2. These freedoms are subject only to such limitations as are prescribed by law and necessary in a democratic society in the interests of protecting:
   - public order, health or morals;
   - rights and freedoms of others;
   - public safety.
3. There is an absolute right to freedom of thought, conscience and religion as these are personal internal matters and cannot practically be restricted, but the freedom to *manifest* them is qualified because of the above restrictions.
4. There is a wide range of rights (not restricted to traditional religious views) protected by Article 9 included in the following (chronological) list:
   - pacifism (*Arrowsmith v UK* (1978));
   - Scientology (*X and Church of Scientology v Sweden* (1979));
   - Islam (*Ahmad v UK* (1982));
   - Druidism (*Chappell v UK* (1987));
   - Jehovah's Witnesses (*Hoffman v Austria* (1993));

- veganism (*X v UK* (1993));
- the Krishna Movement (*Iskon v UK* (1994)).

5. Views not coming within the scope of the article include:
   - political beliefs (*McFeeley v UK* (1980));
   - pure altruistic ideals (*Vereniging Rechtswinkels Utrecht v Netherlands* (1986)).

6. The 'manifestation' aspects are important because they can cause disharmony so qualifications preclude:
   - convincing one's neighbour of one's beliefs (*Kokkinakis v Greece* (1993));
   - giving conscientious objectors the right to avoid military service by alternative activities (*N v Sweden* (1984));
   - conscientious objection to observance of municipal obligations such as being bound by planning restrictions (*Iskon v UK* (1994)) or making maintenance order payments (*Karakuzey v Germany* (1996)).

7. A careful balance is needed when the question of proselytism arises between the interests of the would-be converter and the potential convertee (*Kokkinakis v Greece* (1993)).

7.1.11 Freedom of expression (Article 10)

1. Extends to freedom to hold opinions or receive and impart information and ideas without interference by public authority and regardless of frontiers.

2. It does not prevent states from requiring licensing of broadcasting, television or cinema enterprises.

3. Qualification of this freedom is justified in Article 10 because its exercise carries with it duties and responsibilities so it may be subject to such formalities, conditions, restrictions or penalties as are prescribed by law and necessary in a democratic society in the interests of:
   - national security, territorial integrity or public safety;
   - prevention of disorder or crime;
   - protection of health or morals;
   - protection of the reputation or rights of others;

- preventing disclosure of information received in confidence;
- maintaining the authority and impartiality of the judiciary.

4. 'Expression' includes rights to:
   - free speech;
   - press freedom;
   - receive information and find out about things via diverse media including radio, television, film, telephone, and the web;
   - protection for people doing this, eg by journalists not revealing sources and professional persons maintaining client confidentiality.

5. Freedom of expression is important because it is a prerequisite for the enjoyment of other rights and freedoms and is thus widely interpreted to cover various kinds of expression, political and artistic, commercial, public and private.

6. Case law exemplifies this, eg:
   - allowing questioning (but not denying the existence) of historical events such as the holocaust (*Lehideux and Isorni v France* (1998));
   - protesting against other people's activities even where this might involve some interference eg blood sports (*Hashman and Harrup v UK* (2000));
   - preventing attempts to hold secret inquiries into matters of public concern such as the Shipman murders (*R (Wagstaff) v Sec of State for Health* (2001));
   - press freedom to report celebrity events (*Douglas v Hello!* (2001));
   - right of prisoners to communicate with the press (*R (Simms) v Secretary of State for the Home Dept* (2000)).

7. The media can use public interest to justify matters published and if acting in good faith are entitled to rely on the truth of quotations and extracts from other apparently reliable sources such as official reports.

7.1.12 Freedom of assembly and association (Article 11)

1. Freedom of peaceful assembly and association with others includes the right to form and join trades unions for protection, with no restrictions to be placed on such freedoms other than as prescribed by law and necessary in a democratic society in the interests of:
   - national security or public safety;
   - prevention of disorder or crime;
   - protection of health or morals;
   - protection of the rights and freedoms of others.
2. Under Article 11 states can impose lawful restrictions on the exercise of rights:
   - by members of the armed forces;
   - by police;
   - in the course of state administration.
3. These freedoms are connected to and are extensions of Article 10 rights to freedom of expression and assemblies can include:
   - marches and demonstrations (*Christians Against Racism v UK* (1980));
   - being in locations where obstruction might be occasioned, such as the public highway (*Rassemblement Jurassien and Unite Jurassiene v Switzerland* (1979) and *Jones & Lloyd v DPP* (1999)).
4. Provided that restrictions imposed are lawful, necessary and proportionate, it is legitimate for states to restrict the right to peaceful assembly in order to:
   - prevent the occurrence of disorder (*Choherr v Austria* (1993));
   - ban meetings and marches in extreme circumstances provided they are not complete banning orders (*Rai and others v UK* (1995)).
5. With regard to the right of association other established rules are that:

- political parties come within its scope (*United Communist Party of Turkey v Turkey* (1998));
- prisoners (*McFeeley v UK* (1980)) and professional regulatory bodies (*Revert v France* (1989)) usually will not;
- political activities of state security forces such as the police are acceptable so long as this is in the public interest (*Rekvenyi v Hungary* (1999)).

7.1.13 Obligation to respect human rights (Article 1) and right to an effective remedy (Article 13)

Both these fundamental rights are excluded from the HRA as the enactment itself satisfies Article 1 and the courts' ability to provide a remedy for Convention breaches under section 8 of the Act is thought to satisfy Article 13.

7.1.14 Prohibition of discrimination (Article 14)

1. This article's comprehensive and unqualified provisions state that the enjoyment of the rights and freedoms set forth in the Convention shall be secured without discrimination on any ground such as sex, race, colour, language, religion, political or other opinion, national or social origin, association with a national minority, property, birth or other status.
2. Under the *eiusdem generis* statutory interpretive rule protection is not restricted to these categories because of the use of the words 'such as' and 'or other status' the latter applying to:
   - imprisonment;
   - conscientious objection;
   - marital and professional status;
   - trades union activities;
   - illegitimacy.
3. Comparisons must be fair and equivalent, judicial decisions stating that:

- it is not discrimination to treat married and unmarried couples differently, as they have different legal status (*Lindsay v UK* (1986));
- trainee barristers are different from trade apprentices (*Van der Mussele v Belgium* (1983));
- justification that discrimination is in the public interest must be convincing (*Larkos v Greece* (1999);
- mere administrative convenience for the state will not succeed (*Darby v Sweden* (1990)).

4. Discrimination particularly disliked by the judiciary includes:
   - race (*East African Asians v UK* (1973));
   - denial of sexual equality (*Abdulaziz and others v UK* (1985));
   - illegitimacy (*Inze v Austria* (1987));
   - religion (*Hoffmann v Austria* (1993));
   - nationality (*Gaygusuz v Austria* (1996)).

5. Positive discrimination may be acceptable, eg:
   - *Belgian Linguistic Case* (1968);
   - tax legislation favourable to women to persuade them into employment (*Lindsay v UK* (1986)).

6. Rights encompassed by Article 14 are available in conjunction with the other Convention rights rather than being separate and self-standing.

7.2 The Convention Protocols

7.2.1 The Protocols

All states were not ready to accept everything in 1950 so some elements were promulgated by later Protocols including:

- rights to property, education and free elections (Protocol 1 Articles 1, 2 and 3);
- prohibition of imprisonment for debt (Protocol 4 Article 1);
- freedom of movement, prohibition of expulsion of nationals and collective expulsion of nationals (Protocol 4 Articles 2, 3 and 4);
- Protocol 6 dealing with the death penalty;

- Various provisions in Protocol 7 on criminal appeals, compensation, double jeopardy and equality between spouses.

7.2.2 Protection of property (Protocol 1 Article 1)

1. Protocol 1 provides that every natural and legal person (ie people and corporations) is entitled to peaceful enjoyment of his or its possessions; no one is to be deprived of them except in the public interest and subject to conditions provided for by law and general principles of international law.

2. This does not deprive states of the right to enforce such laws as they deem necessary to control the use of property in accordance with the general interest or to secure payment of taxes or other contributions or penalties.

3. Legal and natural persons may be entitled to human property rights eg limited liability companies and corporations so a *company's* 'human rights' were breached when there was undue delay in reaching a decision following a public inquiry into a plan to quarry on the Scottish island of South Harris (*Re Lafarge Redland Aggregates Ltd* (2000)).

4. A number of different types of human rights violations can be identified although property rights often arise in conjunction with other substantive rights including:
   - inequitable treatment of men vis-à-vis women in respect of social security benefits to which they were disentitled as widowers but would have been entitled were they widows (*Leary v UK* (2000) and *Cornwell v UK* (2000));
   - expropriation of assets of a human person (*National & Provincial Building Society etc. v UK* (1997) or legal person (*Air Canada v UK* (1995)).

5. Property rights to which the Protocol refers cover a wide range of subject matter, the European Commission and Court having identified:
   - shares (*Bramelid and Malstrom v Sweden* (1982));
   - goodwill (*Van Marle v Netherlands* (1986));
   - fishing rights (*Baner v Sweden* (1989));

- patents (*Smith Kline and French Laboratories Ltd v Netherlands* (1990));
- ownership of debts or claims (*Greek Refineries etc v Greece* (1994));
- licences (*IS v Netherlands* (1995)).

6. Social engineering and the necessity of maintaining a fair balance between political objectives was tested in *James v UK* (1986) where the Duke of Westminster challenged the Leasehold Reform Act 1967 provisions forfeiting the reversion of long leases in favour of tenants who would otherwise have had their homes confiscated, the decision being that the legislation was justified.

7. The limitation rules relating to adverse possession of land were unsuccessfully challenged in *Family Housing Association v Donnellan and Others* (2002) which held that:
   - they were rules of private law and outside the scope of the Convention;
   - the purpose was to prevent expropriation of private property by the state;
   - the 12-year limitation period is adequate to allow dispossessed persons to assert ownership rights.

8. The cases of *Pye (Oxford) Ltd v UK* (2007) and *Beaulane Properties v Palmer* (2006) confirm that human rights legislation applies to adverse possession of land.

7.2.3 Right to education (Protocol 1 Article 2)

1. No one should be denied the right to education, and in the exercise of any functions assumed by the state relating to education and teaching, it shall respect the right of parents to ensure such education and teaching is in conformity with their own religious and philosophical aims.

2. However the UK entered a reservation because certain provisions of UK education legislation only required educational services to be provided if they were compatible with provision of efficient instruction and training and avoidance of unreasonable public expenditure.

3. The government maintained this stance in 1998 and so kept the reservation when enacting the HRA.

4. The Protocol operates to provide a positive, practical and effective right of access to education, despite its negative wording, so delivery must be in an appropriate language with official recognition of the qualifications to be obtained (*Belgian Linguistics Case* above).

5. The right can be enforced by:
   - application of punitive provisions to parents who refuse to comply with compulsory schooling requirements (*Family H v UK* (1984));
   - disregarding the beliefs of persons other than parents where they have custody of the child, eg adoptive parents (*X v UK* (1977)).

6. States must also respect parents' religious and philosophical convictions:
   - this extends beyond education into areas such as discipline by corporal punishment (*Campbell and Cosans v UK* (1982));
   - respecting parents' views does not mean they must be followed or observed, as in choosing single or both sex schooling (*W and others v UK* (1984)).

7. The right to access to education is consistent with the right to establish and run private as well as state schools (*Kjeldson, Busk Madsen and Pederson v Denmark* (1976)), although state regulation of private schools in order to maintain standards by preventing them from teaching without adequate qualified staff is acceptable (*Jordebo v Sweden* (1987)).

8. The distinction between teaching and indoctrination is not always easy to make, but all schools whether state or private can teach subject matter which includes material that conflicts with the strict religious or philosophical beliefs of parents, provided this is done objectively, and opposition to school sex education can be overruled in those circumstances (*Kjeldson et al v Denmark* (1976)).

7.3 Procedure

Adapted from D Gomien, D Harris, L Zwaak, Law and practice of the European Convention on Human Rights and the European Social Charter, *(1996) Council of Europe*

CHAPTER 8

The Human Rights Act

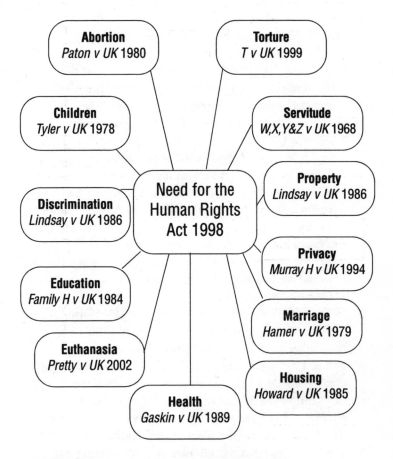

8.1 The European years 1950–98

1. In 1950 the ECHR established the first regional system allowing individuals to bring actions against states, coming into force in 1953, but the UK did not incorporate the

Convention into domestic law, believing there already existed adequate domestic rights and remedies such as:

- habeas corpus;
- jury trial;
- protection against double jeopardy;
- judicial review.

2. After 1966 individuals were permitted to bring cases against the state but the British government's poor record demonstrated that more protection was needed eg in:

- *Hamer v UK* (1979) and *Draper v UK* (1980) the Commission ruled that it was an interference with Article 12 rights and served no legitimate state objectives or interests to prevent prisoners from marrying;
- *Silver v UK* (1983) the whole panoply of UK procedures and remedies – prison board of visitors, ombudsman, Home Secretary and judicial review – failed to remedy a Sikh prisoner's claim that his correspondence had been unlawfully interfered with contrary to Article 8 of the Convention;
- *Malone v UK* (1984) the common law failed to protect British citizens against police telephone tapping, leading to the enactment of the Interception of Communications Act 1985.

3. In the mid-1990s the Labour Party pledged reform, and the Court and Commission were replaced from 1 November 1998 by a reconstituted full-time Court.

4. Before 1998 UK courts accepted there was a presumption that legislation would not intentionally breach the Convention (*Re M and H (Minors)* (1990)) but there was relatively little interest in the European rights approach and a preference for English ideas of civil liberties.

5. However, the HRA was enacted in 1998, coming into effect in October 2000, to allow time for adjustment and training, and it:

- provided that existing UK domestic law would be interpreted, and future law enacted and interpreted, by government and courts in accordance with the

Convention;
- enabled citizens to enforce Convention rights directly in domestic courts.

8.2 Bringing Rights Home 1996

1. Various British historical events and documents have rights and liberty connotations eg:
   - Magna Carta 1215 (rights to jury trial and due process);
   - Bill of Rights 1688 (shifting balance of power from Crown to Parliament).
2. Britain's philosophical writing tradition is extensive and includes:
   - John Locke (*Two Treatises on Government*);
   - Thomas Paine (*Rights of Man*);
   - John Stuart Mill (*On Liberty*).
3. Historically other factors besides lost cases fuelled the need for change, eg:
   - xenophobic legislation such as the:
     - Aliens Acts of 1905 and 1914;
     - Commonwealth Immigrants Acts of 1962 and 1968;
     - immigration statutes of the 1990s;
   - Registration of Business Names Act 1916;
   - increasing power of the executive at the expense of legislature and judiciary.
4. A long-standing campaign by various people over several decades eventually led to a 1996 consultation paper *Bringing Rights Home* being published, followed by a White Paper *Rights Brought Home: The Human Rights Bill* (Cm 3782) which:
   - made the case for change;
   - explained the government's proposals for enforcing Convention rights;
   - indicated how this would improve compliance;
   - set out derogations and reservations which the government considered necessary.

8.3 The Human Rights Act 1998

8.3.1 Further effect to the Convention

1. The HRA gives 'further effect' to the Convention in a number of ways, section 2(1) stating that for interpretation of Convention rights, courts and tribunals must take into account:
   - European Court judgments, decisions, declarations or advisory opinions;
   - Commission reports and decisions;
   - Decisions of the Committee of Ministers.

2. For interpreting domestic legislation section 3(1) provides that Acts of Parliament and subordinate legislation (statutory instruments, bye-laws etc) must be read so far as possible compatibly with Convention rights, with the qualification that this does not affect the validity, operation or enforcement of pre-existing legislation.

3. The higher courts are empowered to make 'declarations of incompatibility' under section 4 where in any proceedings dealing with primary legislation the Court is satisfied that some provision is incompatible with Convention rights.

4. The higher courts are:
   - House of Lords;
   - Judicial Committee of the Privy Council;
   - Courts Martial Appeal Court;
   - Scottish High Court of Justiciary sitting otherwise than as a trial court or the Court of Session;
   - High Court;
   - Court of Appeal.

5. Where any of these courts is considering making a declaration of incompatibility notice should be given to the Crown so that the relevant minister or nominee can be joined as a party to the proceedings.

6. The law may then be amended and failure to do so would lead to probable action in the European Court with the government eventually losing, accompanied by bad

publicity.

7. Lower courts lack this power and must follow the legislation, nor can they trigger the section 10 remedial order provisions providing a fast track procedure to amend defective legislation; lower courts include county and magistrates' courts and other tribunals.

8.3.2 Incompatibility and illegality

Incompatibility

1. An early example of a declaration of incompatibility was *H v Mental Health Review Tribunal N & E London Region* (2001) concerning the burden of proof on patients seeking release in applications to Mental Health Review Tribunals.

2. Following this case the government were obliged to take the following steps:
   - a remedial order was made in November 2001;
   - retrospective approval was granted by Parliament in April 2002;
   - patients subjected to similar injustice could claim compensation.

3. Public authorities are courts, tribunals and any person certain of whose functions are of a public nature.

4. Obligation is imposed on public authorities to act compatibly with Convention rights under section 6.

5. Parliament and its activities are excluded.

Illegality

1. Where the Court finds the act of a public authority unlawful, section 8 authorises:
   - such relief, remedy, or order as it considers just and appropriate;
   - power to award damages, with some restrictions.

2. Public authorities include:
   - those legislatively designated ie courts and tribunals (section 6);
   - others whose functions are obviously public eg:
     - government departments;

- local authorities;
- police and prison services;
- hybrids eg housing associations (*Poplar Housing and Regeneration Community Association v Donoghue* (2001));
- non-hybrid bodies eg charities (*R (on the application of Heather) v Leonard Cheshire Foundation* (2003);

3. Convention rights to which the Act gives further effect mean:
   - rights and fundamental freedoms set out in Articles 2–12 and 14 of the Convention;
   - Articles 1-3 of the First Protocol;
   - Articles 1 and 2 of the Sixth Protocol as read with Articles 16–8 of the Convention, subject to any designated reservation or derogation, as enacted by section 1 HRA.

8.3.3 Structure of the Human Rights Act Chapter 42

The Act comprises 22 sections and three schedules.

The Human Rights Act 1998

Introduction

s. 1   The Convention Rights

s. 2   Interpretation of Convention rights

Legislation

s. 3   Interpretation of legislation

s. 4   Declaration of incompatibility

s. 5   Right of Crown to intervene

Public authorities

s. 6   Acts of public authorities

s. 7   Proceedings

s. 8   Judicial remedies

s. 9   Judicial acts

Remedial action

s. 10   Power to take remedial action

Other rights and proceedings

s. 11   Safeguard for existing human rights

s. 12   Freedom of expression

s. 13   Freedom of thought, conscience and religion

Derogations and reservations

s. 14   Derogation

s. 15   Reservation

s. 16   Period for which designated derogations have effect

s. 17   Periodic review of designated reservations

Judges of the European Court of Human Rights

s. 18   Appointment to European Court of Human Rights

Parliamentary procedure

s. 19   Statements of compatibility

Supplemental

s. 20   Orders etc under this Act

s. 21   Interpretation

s. 22   Short title, commencement, application and content

Schedules

Schedule 1 The articles

Part I The Convention rights and freedoms

Sets out the rights and freedoms contained in Convention Articles 2–12, 14, and 16–8, from the right to life to limitations on the use of restrictions on rights (see the previous chapter on the Convention for more detail of the actual articles).

Part II The First Protocol

Articles 1–3 deal with protection of property, the right to education and free elections; Part II of the HRA sets out the reservation made in 1952 to the right to education, article 2 being accepted by the UK only so far as it is compatible with the provision of efficient instruction and training, and the avoidance of unreasonable public expenditure.

Part III The Sixth Protocol

Article 1 abolishes the death penalty and article 2 allows states to make provision for the death penalty in times of war or imminent threat of war.

Schedule 2 Remedial orders

Section 10 of the Act gives power to take remedial action where legislation has been declared under section 4 to be incompatible with a Convention right, and this schedule makes further provision on procedure, urgent cases and definitions for such action under section 10(7).

Schedule 3 Derogation and reservation

This schedule explains why the UK has derogated (Part I) or made reservations (Part II) from the Convention, the derogation relating to terrorism measures introduced by the government in 1974 arising from the Northern Ireland disturbances and the adverse European Court's decision of *Brogan and others* in 1988.

Schedule 4 Judicial pensions

This obliges the appropriate Minister to ensure that there are pension provisions for any holder of a judicial office who serves as a European Court judge, with statutory instruments providing rules in connection with the HRA.

8.4 Current issues

8.4.1 Right to life

1. Causes conflict between:
   - law;
   - morality;
   - ethics;
   - religion;
   - human rights.
2. This inter-connectedness was demonstrated in *Airedale NHS Trust (Respondents) and Bland (Appellant)* (1993) where law lords' speeches concerning teenage football fan Anthony Bland, in a persistent vegetative state (PVS) because of a stadium collapse, called on moral philosophy to help conclude that it is permissible to terminate medical treatment and nourishment when all hope of meaningful life is gone.
3. Cases such as *NHS Trust A v M* and *NHS Trust B v H* (2001) confirm that where patients are in a PVS their right to life is not infringed by withdrawal of treatment.
4. In the case of conjoined twins Jodie and Mary (*Re A (Children) (Conjoined Twins: Surgical Separation)* (2001) the:
   - Catholic parents' preferred alternative was inaction so that nature could take its course;
   - Court of Appeal held that the paramount interests of the child should prevail, even though that meant sacrificing one of the infant lives.
5. In Diane Pretty's case her views were known, unlike the two previous ones, and three Convention articles were considered and rejected by the courts (*Pretty v UK* (2002)):
   - Article 3 (inhuman and degrading treatment);
   - Article 8 (right to privacy);
   - Article 14 (right not to be discriminated against).

6. State law can be amended to achieve humane results in such instances eg euthanasia laws in the Netherlands and Switzerland, but this has not been done in the UK despite attempts by private members bills.

8.4.2 Right to privacy

Protecting individual rights
1. Privacy questions arise in various circumstances:
   * rights of 'ordinary' citizens;
   * celebrities' hurt pride or economic interests;
   * protection of criminals;
   * protection of reputations.
2. Examples include:
   * *Douglas v Hello!* (2001) where two actors indirectly obtained recognition of their right to privacy by the Court of Appeal developing the common law of breach of confidence;
   * two child killers obtained court orders preventing the media from disclosing their whereabouts on release from prison (*Thompson and Venables v News Groups Newspapers* (2001));
   * Maxine Carr, former girlfriend of murderer Ian Huntley, was granted police protection and a new identity on her release from prison.
3. Footballer Garry Flitcroft tried to prevent publication of allegations of adultery with two women but an injunction was refused (*A v B (a company)* (2002)).
4. The duty of confidence arises where the person(s) subject to the duty (in these cases the media) know or ought to know that the 'victim' reasonably expects to be protected against disclosure.
5. In Jamie Theakston's case he could not prevent publication of reports of his visiting a brothel although he did prevent photographs being published as permission ought reasonably to be given for such publication (*Theakston v Mirror Group Newspapers* (2002)).
6. In another case the Court of Appeal indicated that:

- the fact of a person's being in public life does not of itself mean that any aspect of it can be published;
- if the public person chooses to lie (in her case about drug addiction) the press may be allowed to set the record straight (*Naomi Campbell v Mirror Group Newspapers* (2003)).

ID cards

1. Wider questions of public interest arise and in November 2003 the Home Secretary announced that the government intended to introduce a national identity cards scheme following a consultation period in the previous year with various implications:
   - publication of a draft bill in mid-2003 reignited concerns about the purpose, scope and human rights implications;
   - the government's own Information Commissioner told MPs he was increasingly alarmed by the proposals;
   - the Identity Cards Act received royal assent on 30 March 2006;
   - the Home Office says they will introduce biometric residence permits for foreign nationals in 2008 and they expect the first ID cards to be issued to British citizens in 2009.
2. Arguments against the use of ID cards are that:
   - they can be used oppressively by totalitarian governments, possible even in a democracy;
   - governments might extend the range of uses to which they put the data bases which comprise the brain and memory behind the cards;
   - security cannot be guaranteed and government has a poor record of protecting confidential data.
3. Biometric identification has unfortunate resonances with Nazi and apartheid regimes and suggested drawbacks are that:
   - misuse could restrict, control or remove rights of privacy and freedom of movement;

- tracing terrorists might be followed by tracing criminals ranging from murderers, bank robbers and paedophiles through speeding motorists to people who talk on telephones in their cars or drop sweet papers in the street;
- government has an appalling record for mismanaging and overspending on large computerisation programmes eg the Millennium Dome, immigration, passports, NHS reforms and the Scottish Parliament.

4. Introduction of restrictions eg for passports from:
- 2007 applicants aged 11+ years have to prove their identity in person;
- 2009 finger printing and recording on biometric database;
- once on the database moving home without informing the authorities risks a £1,000 fine.

5. Properly managed, bringing together different forms of ID might be more convenient for government and citizens, if distrust of government could be overcome and guarantees provided against misuse. However, there are grave and unresolved doubts about both technology and government's ability to handle this.

8.4.3 Fair trial

Requisites of fair trial

1. The right to a fair trial involves a wide panoply of issues only touched upon in the Convention but which include:
- pre-trial rights such as prohibition of arbitrary arrest and detention;
- knowledge of the accusation;
- rights to professional representation and prompt appearance before a judicial tribunal;
- detention under humane conditions and a prohibition on being held incommunicado.

2. Hearings require:
- fairness;

- publicity;
- competent representation and impartiality of tribunal;
- presumption of innocence and adequate time to prepare a defence followed by speedy trial, rights to examine witnesses and obtain the services of a competent interpreter;
- prohibitions on self-incrimination, retrospective criminal sanctions, and double jeopardy.

3. Post-trial rights include the right to:
   - appeal;
   - compensation for miscarriages of justice;
   - absence of delay in rectifying injustices.

Inroads into fair trials

1. Some of these rights have been strained or restricted recently eg:
   - resulting from terrorism or combating crime;
   - implementing cheaper procedures;
   - removing some trials from jurors who may not understand complex cases.
2. Under the Criminal Justice Act 2003:
   a) section 43 deals with applications by the prosecution for certain fraud cases to be conducted without a jury in serious or complex matters:
      - the judge can make an order where the length and/or complexity of the trial is likely to make it so burdensome to the jury that the interests of justice require this to be done;
      - the Lord Chief Justice or his nominated judge must approve the arrangement;
   b) the principle of double jeopardy is breached ie the rule that people should not be tried twice for the same offence and once acquitted that should be an end to the matter *(autrefois acquit)*;
   c) section 75 allows certain cases to be retried and the following sections 76–83 cover applications for retrial with section 84 referring to the retrial itself;

    d) the Fraud (Trials without Jury) Bill 2007 proposed to remove section 43 amidst extensive opposition in the House of Lords and it is possible that further changes in the law reducing the protection provided by juries may be enacted.

3. The original rationale of fairness to the accused is counter-balanced by the argument that modern scientific and forensic investigatory methods mean that evidence may still be available after an acquittal years ago which today would be sufficient to convict.

4. Human rights considerations include:
   - need for certainty and closure;
   - fallibility and misuse of scientific evidence.

8.4.4 Terrorism

Aspects of terrorism

1. Terrorist threats provide government with cogent reasons to curtail liberty, to be weighed against moral ideas of what is right and fair and the provisions of the Convention and domestic law.

2. Emergency powers have been exercised under English law for centuries and are used to address contemporary threats perceived or real:
   - habeas corpus allowing an accused to be brought before the courts can be suspended, although the last occasion was in Ireland between 1866 and 1869;
   - martial law is an extreme form of military rule when the army takes over in times of war or grave disturbance, not used in Britain since 1780 but implemented in Ireland from 1916 to 1920;
   - emergency powers were used during both world wars and may still be invoked by government to combat terrorism.

The Terrorism Act 2000

1. The present UK legal definition is contained in section 1 of the Terrorism Act 2000 and it:

- comprises threats or actions involving serious violence to people or property which endangers life and creates serious risks to public health or safety;
- includes interference or disruption to electronic systems where the objective is to intimidate or coerce governments or people in order to advance political, religious or ideological causes;
- thus comprises a raft of activities, threats and objectives, wide but not all embracing.
2. Excluded is ordinary political protest designed to change government's behaviour eg:
   - anti-tax increase campaigns;
   - trade and industrial disputes.
3. Neither of these involves the gratuitous and random violence that frequently accompanies terrorist activities often characterised by:
   - indifference to human life;
   - hatred of people with different beliefs;
   - religious, cultural or political agendas.
4. Such factors are used by government to justify stringent and sometimes repressive measures which themselves violate normally accepted standards of human rights eg detention without trial.
5. Objectives of the Terrorism Act 2000 were to:
   - reform terrorism law;
   - establish procedures proscribing illegal organisations;
   - make fundraising provisions;
   - tackle money laundering;
   - improve investigatory procedures.

Anti-terrorism, Crime and Security Act 2001

1. The 2000 Act came into force in February 2001 but the attack on the twin towers in New York on 11 September 2001 (commonly referred to as '9/11') led to the Anti-terrorism, Crime and Security Act 2001 with 129 sections, 14 parts and 8 schedules.

2. Provisions covered by the 2001 Act include:
   - forfeiture of terrorist cash and the Treasury's ability to freeze assets, sections 1 and 4;
   - denial of refugee status to certain groups of people, sections 33 and 34;
   - introduction of criminal liability for making, possessing or exploding nuclear weapons, section 47.
3. Persons suspected by the Home Secretary of being terrorists but who cannot be returned to a country where they might be tortured or killed can be detained indefinitely:
   - appeal is to the Special Immigration Appeals Commission (SIAC) which deals with appeals from Home Office decisions to deport or exclude people from the UK on national security grounds or for other public interest reasons;
   - the suspect and his lawyer are not entitled to see evidence and can be excluded from the hearing if the material is deemed to be secret;
   - this is an Article 15 derogation from the Article 5 right not to be arbitrarily detained, justified by perception that there is a threat of war or sufficiently severe public emergency;
   - the House of Lords ruled on 16 December 2004 that indefinite detention without trial of foreign nationals under emergency terror laws is incompatible with European human rights laws (*A(FC) and others v Home Secretary* (2004)).
4. Part 3 of the Act allows the police to:
   - seek private and personal information without warrant or disclosing the fact, by going through government and public department files;
   - claim that it might be useful to an investigation whether or not they are likely to find evidence of criminal activities.
5. Under section 89 the powers already available in the Police and Criminal Evidence Act 1984 and Terrorism Act 2000

are extended to allow more fingerprinting and retention of records that formerly would have been destroyed.

6. Under Part 12:
   - the previous practice of using telephone data for billing and then destroying it is removed;
   - records must be retained in case they might prove useful in the investigation of future offences;
   - confidentiality is thus removed from telephonic communications.

Prevention of Terrorism Act 2005

1. The 2005 Act:
   - replaces Part 4 powers under the Anti-terrorism, Crime and Security Act 2001;
   - introduces control orders to be made against suspected terrorists whether UK or foreign;
   - responded to the condemnation of the government by the House of Lords for unlawful detention of suspects in *A(FC) and others v Home Secretary* (2004).

2. Under section 1 the Home Secretary or court can make a control order imposing obligations on an individual including prohibiting or restricting:
   - possession or use of specified articles;
   - using specified services or facilities or carrying on activities;
   - occupation, work or business;
   - association or communications with others;
   - residence and who is allowed access;
   - where and when he can be away from his address;
   - movement within or from the UK.

3. Other restrictions include surrender of passport, allowing search of premises and photographing of suspect and reporting where and when ordered to do so.

4. Control orders are of two kinds, namely those which do or do not require derogation from the Convention:
   - non-derogating orders are made by the Secretary of State;

- derogating orders are made by the Court on the Secretary's application.

5. The Secretary of State has to report periodically to Parliament on control orders, and the working of the Act is monitored by an independent expert who reported in 2007 that the control order system remains essential but sometimes obligations imposed are more cautious and extensive than absolutely necessary.

6. Up to the date of the second report in 2007 there were:
   - 19 controlees;
   - six were quashed by the Court of Appeal but new orders were made for five and one absconded;
   - three other controlees absconded in the early months of 2007.

7. The system is under challenge: *Home Secretary (Respondent) v MB (FC) (Appellant; Home Secretary (Appellant) v JJ and others (Respondents); Home Secretary (Respondent) v AF (Appellant)* (heard 5-13 July 2007 on which the House of Lords issued their verdicts on 31 October 2007).

8. In summary the:
   - 2004 House of Lords' decision confirmed contravention of the Human Rights Act by illegal detention without trial;
   - Prevention of Terrorism Act 2005 provided control orders designed to detain suspects with conditions under house arrest;
   - 31 October 2007 House of Lords' verdicts ordered a further partial rethink of the control order provisions by the government, saying that an 18 hour per day restriction was an infringement of the controlee's human right to liberty but that a 12 hour per day restriction could be acceptable;
   - the Home Secretary's immediate response was that she would seek to introduce a 16 hour per day curfew instead.

Serious Organised Crime and Police Act 2005

1. Effectively abolishes arrestable offences and provides constables with power of arrest based on one of the specified grounds:
   - to ascertain the name and/or address of the arrested person where in doubt;
   - to prevent the suspect from causing:
     - physical injury to self or another;
     - loss of or damage to property;
     - unlawful obstruction of the highway.
   - to prevent the suspect from committing an offence against public decency;
   - to protect:
     - the suspect from suffering physical injury;
     - a child or other vulnerable person from the person being arrested.
   - to allow the prompt and effective investigation of the offence or conduct of the person being arrested;
   - to prevent prosecution being hindered by disappearance of the suspect.
2. The Act includes a draconian provision to prevent demonstrations within an exclusion zone of one kilometre from anywhere in Parliament Square.
3. The purpose of this was to remove Brian Haw, an embarrassing five-year peace demonstrator against the Iraq war.
4. The first conviction under the Act was of Maya Evans for the crime of reading out the names of British soldiers and Iraqi civilians killed in the Iraq war.
5. Human rights groups point to this part of the Act as symptomatic of how traditional rights are being trampled under the juggernaut of modern legislation and ill-considered reaction not merely to terrorism but to legitimate opposition.

Terrorism Act 2006

1. This is described as a comprehensive package of measures (compared with the single control order purpose of the Prevention of Terrorism Act 2005) and is intended to provide the police, intelligence agencies and courts with all necessary means to tackle terrorism and bring perpetrators to justice.

2. Major new offences created by Part I of the Act are:
   - encouragement of terrorism (section 1);
   - dissemination of terrorist publications (section 2);
   - preparation of terrorist acts (section 5);
   - training for terrorism (section 6);
   - making and possession of devices and materials (section 9);
   - misuse of devices and materials (section 10) and threatening to use them (section 11);
   - trespassing on nuclear sites (section 12);
   - maximum imprisonment for possessing for terrorist purposes is increased from 10 to 15 years;
   - directors and others involved with a body corporate may incur personal liability (section 18).

3. Part II (sections 21-35) deals with:
   - proscription of terrorist organisations (sections 21 and 22);
   - detention of terrorist suspects (sections 23-25);
   - searches and other investigatory powers (sections 26-33).

4. Section 36 requires the Secretary of State to appoint a reviewer of the operation of the Terrorism Act 2000 and Part I of this Act at least once every 12 months and to report to Parliament.

5. Extensions to existing legislation made by the 2006 Act are:
   - introduction of warrants to enable police searches of property owned or controlled by terrorist suspects;
   - extension of terrorist stop and search powers to bays and estuaries;

- extension of police detention powers after arrest to 28 days, although periods over two days must be approved by judicial authority;
- powers of search at ports are enhanced;
- the proscription regime is strengthened.

6. This law was enacted in response to the 7 July 2005 bombings in London, but the government's wish for 90-day detention was defeated in the Commons as:
- the police made a poor case for it;
- long periods of detention without arrest are inimical to traditional English civil liberties and modern human rights.

Despite this, the government currently proposes to reintroduce a 42-day detention period.

7. The new offence of glorification was also heavily criticised as too wide, as it might well include eg:
- campaigns such as the 1980s anti-apartheid movement;
- Irish celebrations of incidents in their history;
- crimes of incitement to murder or hatred that already exist.

8. The 2006 Act requires no intention or *mens rea* on the part of the accused individual or group, a significant inroad into civil liberty where criminality is based on speech.

CHAPTER 9

Rights and Remedies

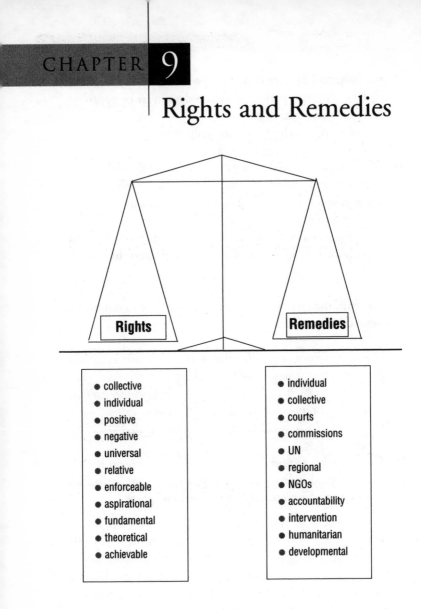

Rights	Remedies
● collective	● individual
● individual	● collective
● positive	● courts
● negative	● commissions
● universal	● UN
● relative	● regional
● enforceable	● NGOs
● aspirational	● accountability
● fundamental	● intervention
● theoretical	● humanitarian
● achievable	● developmental

9.1 Skinning the cat

Ubi jus, ibi remedium: where there is a right, there is a remedy.

9.1.1 Negatives

1. There is more than one way to skin a cat and states develop a variety of remedies and enforcement systems.
2. Article 8 of the Universal Declaration provides that everyone has the right to an effective remedy by competent national tribunals for acts violating their fundamental rights as granted by constitution or law.
3. A remedy is available when an authoritative body – court, legislature or other effective agency – enforces compliance with prescribed norms and/or imposes sanctions for failure so to comply.
4. But in general international law this is problematical because:
   - customary international law is scant and tenuous compared with the common law;
   - international 'legislation' only governs states so far as they choose to be bound by entering into and ratifying treaties;
   - enforcement via the ICJ can only take place when the parties specifically agree to be bound by its jurisdiction and there is no obligatory enforcement mechanism;
   - so if international law is often unclear, unaccepted and unenforceable, how far is it 'law' and where is the 'legal system'?
5. In specific contrast the World Trade Organisation (WTO) is an international legal regime that is enforced more energetically than general international law and human rights, proving that stronger global enforcement is possible.
6. This is because trade is closer to states' self-interest than human rights, which compare poorly with the international law and trade regime because they are:
   - weakly enforceable and enforced;
   - largely aspirational;
   - not the primary focus of most state policy.

9.1.2 Accentuate the positive

1. Nevertheless many rights are more than aspirational because:
   - there is some recognition of limited customary effect of the UN Declaration on Human Rights and the international covenants are widely acknowledged if not always observed;
   - regional regimes have investigatory and/or enforcement machinery;
   - states may have enforceable domestic provisions such as the HRA in the UK.

2. Other enforcement methods are available eg:
   a) specific sanctions through the UN particularly:
      - embargo;
      - exclusion;
      - suspension;
      - military force;
      - expulsion;
   b) accountability may hold individuals responsible via the ad hoc international criminal tribunal system and the International Criminal Court (ICC);
   c) tackling immunity and removing impunity;
   d) use of truth commissions;
   e) intervention;
   f) positive discrimination;
   g) ombudsmen.

3. These differing tools can:
   - alter preconceptions;
   - counteract human rights abuses;
   - sometimes provide and enforce remedies.

9.2 UN enforcement

9.2.1 The Charter

1. Westphalian influence pervades the UN Charter eg:
   - Article 2(4) requires members to refrain from threatening or using force against other states in their international relations;
   - Article 2(7) says that nothing in the Charter authorises UN intervention in state domestic jurisdiction or requires them to submit such matters for UN settlement.
2. Even so the SC sometimes takes action when agreement can be achieved eg the 1999 SC Resolution 1244 authorising implementation of the Kosovo peace settlement enabling the civil presence (*inter alia*) to:
   - perform basic civilian administrative functions;
   - maintain civil law and order and establish local police forces;
   - protect and promote human rights;
   - assure safe and unimpeded return of refugees and displaced persons.
3. UN action is often too little and too late eg Rwanda and Bosnia in the early 1990s and the Darfur massacres of the Sudan in 2003–4 with aggression and displacement still ongoing.
4. UN Charter human rights violation powers may be called 'sanctions' although the Charter does not refer to them as such.
5. Other actions available to the UN include:
   - military force being the most extreme step although rarely used eg the first Gulf War 1990-91;
   - the GA, as advised by the SC, may suspend states under Article 5 of the UN Charter which means loss of membership privileges to the offending member;
   - exclusion under Article 19 of the Charter where a state is in arrears with contributions, although this is not a human rights sanction;

- embargo under Article 41 interferes with an offending state's economic activities which although frequently hitting the wrong targets can:
  - be used in peace or war time;
  - restrict imports or exports of goods;
  - be used as a non-violent method of dealing with a recalcitrant state;
  - deny communications, visitors, and even diplomatic relations.

6. Sanctions may be slow but eventually effective as in South Africa and as a final resort offending states may be expelled or withdraw voluntarily to forestall expulsion.

9.2.2 The International Covenants

1. Implementation of the ICESC is dealt with in Article 2 which contains undertakings from each state party to take steps to realise Covenant rights:
   - individually and through international assistance and cooperation;
   - particularly economic and technical;
   - including requisite state legislation and guarantees of non-discrimination.

2. The ICCPR requires all states to report to the Human Rights Commission (replaced by the Human Rights Council) every five years, and thence to the General Assembly via ECOSOC:
   - indicating which of their domestic laws protect civil and political rights;
   - describing domestic provisions that enhance or inhibit individuals' rights;

3. The Civil and Political Covenant can be implemented in other ways:
   - a state may make an optional Article 41 declaration that another state is abusing civil and political rights which could lead to examination by the former Human Rights Commission but was rarely used;

- under Resolution 1503 of ECOSOC individuals and NGOs can complain of human rights violations by states but these are simply filed unless a considerable number is received in which case the UN has limited power to investigate.

4. Under the optional protocol Article 9 of the Covenant implementation is strengthened in that:
   - the Human Rights Commission (now Council) receives and considers communications from individuals claiming to be victims of violations by Member States;
   - there is no requirement for the exhaustion of local remedies in respect of procedure under the UN Charter;
   - anonymous communications and those abusive of submission rights are inadmissible.

5. Complaints and reporting are not as effective as direct legal enforcement and often the complaints mechanism is not incorporated in a treaty or covenant but must be agreed by individual states under a Protocol, eg in CEDAW.

6. Many UN reports are made by special rapporteurs appointed to investigate particular or generic human rights problems and sometimes NGOs can bring influence to bear.

7. The UN Code of Conduct for Law Enforcement Officials 1979 requires law enforcement officials to:
   - fulfil their legal duties while respecting and protecting human dignity and maintaining and upholding the human rights of all persons;
   - use force proportionately and only when strictly necessary;
   - maintain confidentiality and never use torture or other cruel, inhuman or degrading treatment nor invoke superior orders as an excuse for misbehaviour;
   - protect the health of persons in their custody, combat all corruption, and always respect the Code.

9.3 Accountability

1. The desire for accountability caused the Allies to establish the Nuremberg and Tokyo tribunals after the Second World War, based on assertions that horrendous activities not previously contrary to international law would now be criminal, and introducing genocide and crimes against humanity.
2. Although understandable the tribunals contravened two major rights tenets:
   - they were retrospective;
   - for the Tokyo tribunal, they represented 'victors' justice'.
3. They established a new kind of legal procedure that eventually led via the former Yugoslavia and Rwanda tribunals to the ICC.
4. The need for accountability is demonstrated by crimes committed by heads of state such as:
   - Idi Amin of Uganda;
   - General Pinochet of Chile;
   - General Noriega of Panama;
   - Jean-Bedel Bokassa of the Central African Republic;
   - Pol Pot and the Khmer Rouge.
5. Accountability has connections with:
   - impunity;
   - truth commissions;
   - intervention.

9.4 Impunity

1. Impunity means:
   - exemption or immunity from punishment,
   - recrimination or other unpleasant consequences.

   To act with impunity is to behave in a way that has no consideration for the consequences of one's actions in the belief that you will not have to face adverse repercussions or punishment.

2. It is the arch-enemy of human rights, causing offence to victims, survivors, relatives and all right-thinking citizens, and examples include:
   - avoidance by heads or former heads of state of responsibility for actions undertaken by the state as mentioned above;
   - efforts by states themselves to provide their citizens with blanket protection eg:
     - US insistence on total immunity for its citizens against accusations of war crimes;
     - exclusion of all US citizens from the jurisdiction of the ICC.
3. Impunity can be tackled by:
   - international cooperative efforts to extradite and try alleged criminals;
   - Truth Commissions, used successfully by South Africa and at least 23 other states to bring some closure not likely to result from other legal procedures;
   - states declining to agree to blanket immunity eg the Netherlands, Sweden and Germany's refusal to sign immunity agreements with the United States;
   - continuing the work of the ad hoc tribunals and supporting the ICC.

9.5 Intervention

1. Intervention is:
   - forcible and coercive interference in the internal affairs of a state by one or more other states against the wishes of the intervened state;
   - it includes lesser actions such as sanctions or suspension if they actually have coercive effect.
2. The GA has condemned armed intervention and all other forms of interference or attempted threats against the personality of the state or against its political, economic and cultural elements.

3. The UN Declaration on Principles of International Law concerning Friendly Relations and Cooperation among states (1970) says that no state may use or encourage the use of economic, political or any other type of measures to coerce another state to subordinate its sovereign rights or secure advantages of any kind.

4. Regional treaties such as the Charter of the OAS Article 16 also condemn armed intervention which has been the (often-breached) rule since the Treaty of Westphalia 1648 because states prefer an international order that precludes intervention.

5. The recognition of crimes against humanity, genocide and challenges to impunity mean that intervention is now more likely although Article 2(7) of the UN Charter emphasises that nothing therein authorises the UN to intervene in matters that are essentially within the domestic jurisdiction of any state, the purpose being to maintain sovereignty and territorial integrity.

6. This continues the customary international law position and the principle has been reaffirmed by the GA eg the:
   • Declaration on the Inadmissibility of Intervention (1965);
   • Declaration on Principles of International Law concerning Friendly Relations and Cooperation among states (1970).

7. Nevertheless intervention can occur via three main avenues, ie by:
   • the UN;
   • individual states;
   • coalitions of states.

8. The following will not normally amount to intervention:
   • criticism;
   • diplomatic sanctions;
   • economic sanctions;
   • boycotts eg of sporting events;
   • provision of humanitarian aid if done in accordance with International Red Cross principles and in a non-discriminatory manner.

9. What falls within the domestic jurisdiction of states is not a matter of settled international law but one school of thought argues that the UN Charter read as a whole is sufficient to displace customary law of non-intervention in serious cases eg:
   - Article 1(3) confirms that the UN's purpose is to promote and encourage respect for human rights and fundamental freedoms in the context of achieving international cooperation;
   - Article 55(c) makes similar self-standing provision;
   - Article 56 says that all members pledge themselves to take joint and separate action to achieve protection of human rights.
10. The Vienna Declaration and Programme of Action 1993 was unanimous in stating that the promotion and protection of all human rights is a legitimate concern of the international community.

9.6 Regional enforcement

9.6.1 African Charter

1. Article 30 established the African Commission on Human and Peoples' Rights to promote those rights and ensure their protection in Africa and Article 45 requires the Commission to protect peoples' rights under the Charter conditions.
2. Article 55 authorises African individuals, groups and NGOs to file complaints with the Commission against states that have ratified if they believe violation has occurred.
3. Under Article 58 individuals, indigenous peoples and NGOs may submit complaints alleging a series of serious or massive violations by a state party but domestic remedies must first have been exhausted unless they are ineffective.
4. Practical limits apply to admissibility, eg they must:

- not simply be based on media reports;
- be submitted within a reasonable time;
- not relate to settled cases ie cannot operate as an additional state appeal.
5. Enforceability may be uncertain:
   - decisions are recommendations that states may adopt at their discretion;
   - but the Commission claims its decisions are authoritative interpretations of the Charter and binding on states parties.
6. Following the Commission decision the Assembly of Heads of State and Government decide on further action and decisions remain confidential unless and until this occurs, under Article 59.
7. Final resolution might thus be stifled although the Commission may influence governments behind the scenes and summaries of cases are published in annual reports.
8. The 1998 protocol led to the decision to establish a court whose effectiveness remains to be seen.

9.6.2 The Americas

1. Most states in the Americas accept the compulsory jurisdiction of the Inter-American Court of Human Rights which has reduced if not eliminated human rights violations as acts of state policy, previously a pervasive problem.
2. The two organs that supervise compliance with human rights norms in the region (encompassing North, Central and South America and the Caribbean) are the:
   - Inter-American Court of Human Rights;
   - Inter-American Commission on Human Rights.
3. The Commission's powers are broad compared with the global and other regional systems and include:
   - local visits to states accused of rights violations (visits in loco) which are now of less importance as the main purpose used to be to bring violations to world attention;

- adjudication of cases on its own account (the case system) which is of increasing importance as it allows individuals from OAS Member States to file a petition alleging rights violations with the Commission;
- referring cases to the Court for adjudication although they are relatively few in number but important because individuals cannot directly petition the Court;
- appointing rapporteurs;
- drafting declarations and treaties.

4. Doubts about the effectiveness of the procedures include:
   - criticism of failure to provide due process led to Peru's withdrawing recognition of the Court (illegally, according to the Court);
   - insistence on continuance of the death penalty has led to some states ignoring Court decisions, eg in the Caribbean.

9.6.3 Europe

1. UK law provides various remedies, including:
   - compensation;
   - exemplary and punitive damages;
   - declaratory judgments;
   - habeas corpus;
   - equitable remedies in particular injunction, specific performance and restitution;
   - judicial review.

2. The basic duty in Article 1 of the European Convention requires High Contracting Parties to secure to everyone within their jurisdiction the rights and freedoms defined in section 1 of the Convention with two main complaint procedures:
   - inter-state (Article 33);
   - individual (Article 34).

3. Achievement of these objectives is left to individual states thus:
   - incorporation is not essential;

- responsibility remains with the state so complaints cannot be made against individuals for alleged human rights violations.

4. The right of individual petition is important as it:
   - makes individuals effective subjects of international law in addition to states;
   - allows for enforcement of rights at domestic and European level.

5. The right to an effective domestic remedy is contained in Article 13 based on Article 8 of the Universal Declaration and says that everyone whose Convention rights are violated shall have an effective remedy before a national authority notwithstanding that the violation has been committed by persons acting in an official capacity, binding the Convention to the separate state systems.

6. But interpretation of Article 13 is problematical and has led to awkward questions:
   - What is an arguable claim?
   - What kind of a national authority is required? For example, it need not necessarily be a court.
   - Must there be a remedy or an aggregate of remedies?

7. Limitation is also imposed by Article 35 admissibility criteria which say that the Court can only deal with a matter after exhaustion of all domestic remedies. This is subject to a six-month limitation period.

8. Much case law deals with how effective remedies must be and some of the substantive articles make more detailed and specific provision concerning effectiveness eg:
   - Article 5(4) dealing with deprivation of liberty;
   - Article 6(1) governing the right to a fair and public hearing.

9. Certain policies eg the margin of appreciation can lead to difficulties in assessing the effectiveness of human rights in the context of different domestic systems and standards.

Index

Note: ECHR refers to the European
        Convention on Human Rights.

abbreviations 2–3
aboriginal peoples 76–8
abortion 110
accountability 154
adverse possession 124
Afghanistan 67
Africa 82
    African Union (AU) 61
    AU human rights bodies 61–3
    enforcement 157–8
    Organisation of African Unity (OAU)
        60–1
    principal documents 60
    see also individual countries
age, old 55, 58, 115
Albania 74
Americas *see individual countries;*
        Organisation of American States
Anti-terrorism, Crime and Security Act
        2001 103, 141–3
apartheid
    Security Council 34–5
    South Africa 34–5, 89–90
    UN Convention 91
Aquinas, Thomas 20
Arab Declaration and Charter 64–6
Arbour, Louise 33
Argentina 92
ASEAN (Association of South East Asian
        Nations) 66
Asia-Pacific Forum of National Human
        Rights Institutions 66–8
assembly and association, freedom of
    Convention on the Rights of the
        Child 45
    ECHR 120–1
    ICCPR 39
    UDHR 29
Augustine of Hippo, St 20
Austin, John 15
Australia 68
Ayala-Lasso, Jose 33

Bentham, Jeremy 15
Bill of Rights 1689 13, 18, 129
Bosnia 74, 151
Burma (Myanmar) 32, 67

Cambodia 41, 67
capital punishment
    abolition of 81–3
    American Convention on Human
        Rights 1969 58
    Arab Charter on Human Rights 66
    Inter-American Court of Human
        Rights 159
CEDAW (Convention on the
        Elimination of all forms of
        Discrimination against Women)
        1981 21, 43–4, 153
charities 132
children 12
    American Convention on Human
        Rights 1969 57, 58
    Arab Charter on Human Rights 66
    conjoined twins 110, 135
    corporal punishment 111, 125
    ECHR 110, 114, 115–16, 124–5, 135
    education 30, 37, 40, 58, 124–5
    European Convention 1996 107
    European Social Charter 55
    fair trial 114
    family life, right to 115–16
    ICESCR 37, 40
    mistreatment of 22
    slavery and forced labour 80–1
    UN Convention on the Rights of the
        Child 1990 22, 45–6
Chile 93
China 31, 35, 41, 82
CIS Convention on Human Rights 63
claim rights 15
cloning, human 107
Cold War 6, 21, 95
    ICCPR and ICESCR 27, 37
    Security Council 34, 35
collective or group rights 3, 12, 85
colonial states, former 21
common law 96, 128
    breach of confidence 136–7
companies 123
comparative analysis of human rights 6–7
    claim rights and liberty rights 15–16
    collective or individual 12
    moral or legal 14
    natural justice and legal justice 14–15
    positive or negative 13
    right or rights 13
    universal or relative 11–12

will theory or interests theory 16–17
compulsory labour and slavery 79–81
    ECHR 101, 102, 111–12
conceptual approach to human rights 6,
    10–11
conflict of laws 49
conscience and religion, freedom of
        thought
    Convention on the Rights of the Child
        45
    ECHR 117–18
    ICCPR 38
    UDHR 29
conscientious objection 118, 121
control orders 143–4
Convention on Human Rights and
        Biomedicine 1997 107
corporal punishment 111, 125
corporations 123
Cote d'Ivoire 62
Council of Europe
    background 94–7
    Committee of Ministers 98
    institutions 98
    objectives 97–8
    see also European Convention on
        Human Rights; European Court
        of Human Rights
crimes against humanity
    background 83–4, 95–6
    modern position 84–5
Criminal Justice Act 2003 19, 139–40
Croatia 74
Cuba 31, 56
cultural relativism 11–12, 17, 68
customary international law 149, 156

Dark Age 20
De Mello, Sergio Vieira 33
death penalty
    abolition of 81–3
    American Convention on Human
        Rights 1969 58
    Arab Charter on Human Rights 66
    Inter-American Court of Human
        Rights 159
degrading or inhuman treatment see
        torture
Disabilities Convention, UN 47, 74–5
discrimination, prohibition of
    ECHR 121–2
    'jus cogens' 50
    UN Convention on Racial

Discrimination 1969 42–3
divorce 117
double jeopardy 18–19, 66, 139, 140
Dworkin, Ronald 17

East Timor 88
education, right to
    American Convention on Human
        Rights 1969 58
    ECHR 124–5
    ICCPR 37
    ICESCR 37, 40
    UDHR 30
eiusdem generis rule 121
El Salvador 93
elderly persons 55, 58, 115
elections 29, 54
embargoes, UN 35, 152
emergency powers 140
    see also terrorism
employees 12, 54–5
    disputes 114
enforcement
    accountability 154
    African Charter 157–8
    Americas 158–9
    Arab Charter on Human Rights 66
    Europe 159–60
    generally 148–50
    impunity 154–5
    intervention 155–7
    regional 157–60
    UK law 20, 159
    United Nations 151–3
Enlightenment, Age of the 21
equality of arms 114
'erga omnes' 49
Europe, post-Second World War 53,
    94–5
    British response 96–7
    ECHR see European Convention on
        Human Rights
    European response 96
    legacy of war crimes 95–6
    other Conventions 106–7
European Commission on Human Rights
    97, 98
European Convention on Human Rights
    assembly and association, freedom of
        120–1
    categories of rights 100–1
    characteristics 99
    death penalty 82

derogations 103–4, 142
discrimination, prohibition of 121–2
education, right to 124–5
enforcement 159–60
expression, freedom of 118–19
fair trial, right to 113–15
introduction 53–4
liberty and security, right to 112–13, 142, 144
life, right to 82, 101, 110, 135–6
list of rights 109–10
marry, right to 116–17
non-derogable rights 101–2
private and family life 104–5, 115–16
property, protection of 123–4
Protocols 122–5
punishment without law, no 101, 102, 115
qualified rights 102–3, 104–5
reservations 103–4
rights which can be restricted 102
slavery or forced labour, prohibition of 101, 111–12
thought, conscience and religion, freedom of 117–18
torture or inhuman/degrading treatment, prohibition of 101, 110–11
UK involvement 96–7, 99
European Court of Human Rights 98–9
    admissibility criteria 160
    margin of appreciation 105–6, 160
    procedure 126
    proportionality 104–5
    purposive approach 104
    time limit 160
European Court of Justice (ECJ) 71
European Social Charter 54–5
European Union
    background 70
    Council of Europe 98
    external human rights 73–5
    internal human rights 71–3
euthanasia 110, 135–6
Evans, Maya 145
expression, freedom of
    ECHR 118–19
    UDHR 29

fair trial, right to
    current issues 138–40
    ECHR 113–15
    ICCPR 38

UDHR 28
family and private life
    Convention on the Rights of the Child 45
    ECHR 104–5, 115–16
    ICCPR 38
    UDHR 28
first generation rights 8–9
forced labour and slavery 79–81
    ECHR 101, 102, 111–12
France 24, 35, 84
Fraud (Trials without Jury) Bill 2007 140

Gadaffi, Moammar 62
generational theory 8–10
Geneva Conventions 81
genocide
    background 83–4, 96
    'jus cogens' 50
    modern position 84–5
    Security Council 35
    UN Convention 1951 41–2, 84
Germany 41, 93, 94, 155
Gewirth, Alan 17
glossary 3–4
group or collective rights 3, 12, 85
Guatemala 93

Haiti 35
Hart, H.L.A. 17
Haw, Brian 145
heads of state 154, 155
Hobbes, Thomas 16
Hohfeld, Wesley 7, 15
homosexuals 116
housing associations 132
Human Rights Act 1998 99
    Article 13 ECHR 109, 121
    Article 1 ECHR 121
    background 127–9
    current issues 135–47
    derogations and reservations 104, 124–5
    further effect to ECHR 130–2
    higher courts 130
    illegality 131–2
    incompatibility, declaration of 130–1
    lower courts 131
    structure of 133–4
humanitarian intervention 86–8

ICCPR (International Covenant on Civil and Political Rights) 25, 27,

36–9, 81–2, 117
enforcement 152–3
first generation rights 8
ICESCR (International Covenant on
    Economic, Social and Cultural
    Rights) 25, 27, 36–7, 39–40
enforcement 152
second generation rights 9
ID cards 137–8
illegal detention 142, 144
impunity 154–5
incompatibility, declaration of 130–1
India 34
indigenous peoples 76–8
Indonesia 42
inhuman or degrading treatment *see*
    torture
Inter-American *see* Organisation of
    American States
interests theory 16–17
International Bill of Human Rights 11,
    25, 36–7, 40–1
definition of 3
International Court of Justice (ICJ) 149
International Covenant on Civil and
    Political Rights (ICCPR) 25, 27,
    36–9, 81–2, 117
enforcement 152–3
first generation rights 8
International Covenant on Economic,
    Social and Cultural Rights
    (ICESCR) 25, 27, 36–7, 39–40
enforcement 152
second generation rights 9
International Criminal Court (ICC) 25,
    150, 154
US Citizens 155
International Labour Organisation (ILO)
    80
international law 49–50, 149
customary 149, 156
'jus cogens' 41, 49–50
intervention 155–7
Iran 32
Iraq 35
Ireland 140
Israel 35

Japan 41, 42
Jordan 67
judicial review 20
jury trial, right to 139, 140
'jus cogens' 41, 49–50

Kosovo 88, 151

land law 124
League of Nations 25, 77, 79, 96
legal justice 14–15
legal positivism 14–15
Lemkin, Raphael 41, 83
liberalism 21
liberty rights 15–16
liberty and security, right to 28, 38,
    112–13
control orders 144
derogation 142
Libya 31
life, right to
    ECHR 82, 101, 110, 135–6
    ICCPR 81–2
    UDHR 28, 81
limited liability companies 123

Macedonia 74
Magna Carta 1215 13, 18, 129
margin of appreciation 105–6, 160
marry, right to
    ECHR 116–17
    ICCPR 39
    UDHR 29
martial law 140
Marxism 21
mens rea 147
Middle Ages 20
Migrant Workers Convention 1990 46–7
Mill, John Stuart 15
minorities
    ECHR 53
    European Charter for Regional or
        Minority Languages 1992 106
    Framework Convention 1995 106–7
    see also indigenous peoples
minors *see* children
Minsk Convention 63
Mongolia 67
Montenegro 74
moral claims 14
Myanmar (Burma) 32, 67

natural justice 14
negative human rights 13
Nepal 67
Netherlands 136, 155
New Zealand 68
Nigeria 42

North Korea 67
Northern Ireland 103, 111
Nuremberg trials 84, 95, 154

organ/tissue transplants 107
Organisation of American States (OAS)
        55–6
    American Convention on Human
        Rights 1969 57–8, 82
    American Declaration of the Rights
        and Duties of Man 1948 56–7
    Charter 56, 156
    comparisons 59
    Inter-American Commission on
        Human Rights 56, 59, 158–9
    Inter-American Convention on the
        Forced Disappearance of Persons
        1994 58–9
    Inter-American Court of Human
        Rights 158, 159
    principal documents 55
    Organisation for Security and
        Cooperation in Europe (OSCE)
        68–9

Pakistan 31
Palestine 67
passports 138
peace keeping and humanitarian
        intervention 86–8
persistent vegetative state (PVS) 135
personal injuries, serious 115
Peru 159
political
    activities of state security forces 121
    beliefs 118
    parties 121
    protest 141
positive discrimination 122
positive human rights 13
Prevention of Terrorism Act 2005 143–4
prisoners
    association 121
    communication with press 119
    correspondence 128
    discrimination 121
    marriage 116, 128
    suicide 110, 111
privacy, right to 136–8
private and family life
    Convention on the Rights of the Child
        45
    ECHR 104–5, 115–16

ICCPR 38
UDHR 28
professional regulatory bodies 121
property, protection of
    ECHR 123–4
    UDHR 29
proportionality 104–5
proselytism 118
public authorities 131–2
punishment without law, no 101, 102,
        115
purposive approach 104

Qatar 67

Rawls, John 7, 15, 16
regional regimes 51–2
    Africa 60–3, 157–8
    Americas 55–9, 82, 156, 158–9
    Arab Declaration and Charter 64–6
    Asia-Pacific Forum of National Human
        Rights Institutions 66–8
    Europe 52–5, 159–60
    European Union 70–5, 98
    Minsk Convention 63
    Organisation for Security and
        Cooperation in Europe (OSCE)
        68–9
    see also European Convention on
        Human Rights; European Court
        of Human Rights
relativism, cultural 11–12, 17, 68
religion, freedom of thought, conscience
        and
    Convention on the Rights of the Child
        45
    ECHR 117–18
    ICCPR 38
    UDHR 29
remedies
    accountability 154
    African Charter 157–8
    Americas 158–9
    Arab Charter on Human Rights 66
    Europe 159–60
    generally 148–50
    impunity 154–5
    intervention 155–7
    regional 157–60
    UK law 20, 159
    United Nations 151–3
Renaissance 20
retrospectivity, avoidance of 102, 115

Robinson, Mary 33
Roman law 20
Roosevelt, Eleanor 7, 30
Rousseau, Jean Jacques 13
rule of law 17–20
Russia 31, 35, 63, 84
Rwanda 35, 41, 151

sanctions, UN 150, 151–2
Saudi Arabia 31, 82
schools 125
second generation rights 9
security, right to liberty and 28, 38,
         112–13
    control orders 144
    derogation 142
self-determination 37, 53
Serbia 74
Serious Organised Crime and Police Act
         2005 145
Shue, Henry 17
Sierra Leone 88
slavery
    abolition 78–9
    background 78
    definitions 79
    ECHR 101, 111–12
    ICCPR 38
    modern 79–81
    UDHR 28
social security
    American Convention on Human
         Rights 1969 58
    benefits 123
    ICESCR 40
    right to 29
Somalia 22, 35, 62
sources of public international law 49
South Africa 34, 152
    apartheid 34–5, 89–90
    truth commission 92–3, 155
sovereignty, state 86–7
Special Immigration Appeals Commission
         (SIAC) 142
Sri Lanka 32
Stoics 20
subsistence dwellers 12
Sudan 31, 32, 62, 63, 151
suicide 110, 111
Sweden 155
Switzerland 136

teleological approach 104

telephone data 143
terrorism 23
    2000 Act 140–1, 146
    2006 Act 146–7
    Anti-terrorism, Crime and Security Act
         2001 103, 141–3
    aspects of 140
    detention period 147
    glorification 147
    Prevention of Terrorism Act 2005
         143–4
    Serious Organised Crime and Police
         Act 2005 145
theory, human rights
    comparative or contrasting analysis
         6–7, 11–17
    conceptual approach 6, 10–11
    general development of rights 20–3
    practitioners 7
    rule of law 17–20
    'UN' approach 5–6, 8–10
    writers 7
third generation rights 9
Thoreau, Henry 20
thought, conscience and religion, freedom
         of
    Convention on the Rights of the Child
         45
    ECHR 117–18
    ICCPR 38
    UDHR 29
time limits
    European Court of Human Rights 160
Tokyo trials 95, 154
torture and inhuman/degrading treatment
    ECHR 101, 110–11
    European Convention 1987 106
    ICCPR 38
    UDHR 28
    UN Convention 1987 44–5
trade unions 37, 40, 55, 58, 120, 121
transnational corporations 12
transplants, organ/tissue 107
transsexuals 105
truth commissions 92–3, 155
Turkey 74

ubi ius, ibi remedium 148
UDHR see Universal Declaration of
         Human Rights
Uganda 93
'UN' approach to human rights 5–6,
         8–10

United Kingdom 13, 24, 84, 95
  Criminal Justice Act 2003 19, 139–40
  current issues 135–47
  ECHR 96–7, 99, 103, 115, 124–5
  fair trial 138–40
  HRA *see* Human Rights Act 1998
  ID cards 137–8
  life, right to 135–6
  privacy, right to 136–8
  remedies 20, 159
  rule of law 17–20
  Security Council 35
terrorism *see* terrorism
  United Nations 24–5, 48
  Apartheid Convention 91
  CEDAW 1981 21, 43–4, 153
  Charter 25, 26–7, 40, 86–7, 151–2, 156, 157
  Code of Conduct for Law Enforcement Officials 153
  Commission on Human Rights 26, 30–2, 77, 91, 152, 153
  Convention on the Rights of the Child 1990 22, 45–6
  Declaration on Principles of International Law concerning Friendly Relations and Cooperation among States 1970 156
  Declaration on the Right to Development 10
  Disabilities Convention 47, 74–5
  Economic and Social Council (ECOSOC) 26, 27, 77, 152, 153
  General Assembly 33–4, 90, 91, 151, 155, 156
  Genocide Convention 1951 41–2, 84
  High Commissioner for Human Rights 32–3
  Human Rights Council 31–2, 78, 152, 153
  International Law Commission 95
  Migrant Workers Convention 1990 46–7
  Racial Discrimination Convention 1969 42–3
  Security Council 34–6, 86, 151
  special rapporteurs 153
  Torture Convention 1987 44–5
  UDHR *see* Universal Declaration of Human Rights
United States 24, 25, 84, 155
  capital punishment 82

ICC 25, 32, 155
negative rights 13
Security Council 35
UN Convention on the Rights of the Child 22
UN Human Rights Commission 32
war crimes 155
Universal Declaration of Human Rights (UDHR) 25, 81, 149, 150
  civil and political rights 8, 28–9
  duties 30
  economic, social and cultural rights 9, 29–30
  preamble 27–8
  status 30–1
  universal theory 11–12
USSR 41
Uzbekistan 32

Vasak, Karl 8–10
Vienna Convention on the Law of Treaties 1969 41
Vienna Declaration and Programme of Action 1993 157

war crimes 115
  background 83–4, 95–6
  modern position 84–5
  United States 155
Westphalia, Treaty of 4, 20
will theory 17
women
  CEDAW 1981 21, 43–4, 153
  positive discrimination 122
workers 12, 54–5
  disputes 114
World Trade Organisation (WTO) 149

Yugoslavia, former 35

Zimbabwe 31